A Monk In The World

Dear Ronnie —

A joy
to see you
and
know
you.

Love and Shanti,

Richard
Damien

A Monk In The World

✦

Fully Being Your Spiritual Self In Life

Richard Damien

iUniverse, Inc.

New York Lincoln Shanghai

A Monk In The World
Fully Being Your Spiritual Self In Life

iUniverse books may be ordered through booksellers or by contacting:

iUniverse
2021 Pine Lake Road, Suite 100
Lincoln, NE 68512
www.iuniverse.com
1-800-Authors (1-800-288-4677)

ISBN-13: 978-0-595-37608-7 (pbk)
ISBN-13: 978-0-595-82001-6 (ebk)
ISBN-10: 0-595-37608-8 (pbk)
ISBN-10: 0-595-82001-8 (ebk)

Printed in the United States of America

I dedicate this work to my parents, Ben and Shirley Rosenthal, who have always supported me on my path.

Contents

Acknowledgments

I acknowledge the abundance of remarkable teachers in my life who have opened my heart to a rich, deeply felt experience of sharing my light with the world. Most especially:

Jean Ramsbottom
Werner Erhard
Tamara Diaghilev
Jane Roberts and SETH
Russell Scofield
Swami Muktananda
Gurumayi Chidvilasananda

I also thank those who supported and assisted me in putting this book together, including my editor, Marilee Wyman, graphic designer, Anne Twomey, and the iUniverse team. I am also grateful to Lois Barth for her grounded encouragement.

SHALOM
NAM MYOHO RENGE KYO
OM SHANTI OM

Introduction

We are all spiritual beings. As children, we radiate our essence for all to see. Have you ever marveled at a baby's eyes dancing with light or vicariously experienced the wonder of a child walking in nature? As human beings, this spiritual essence within us is our most precious gift.

When I was a child, my sense of wonder and beauty was so great that living on this earth often became a transcendental experience. As I walked down Chicago's streets, I observed multicolored fields of light around people, plants, and animals. My vision resembled Van Gogh's *Starry Night* with its pulsating swirls of color. Gazing at the sky, I discovered particles of fluid energy. The smaller particles merged with the larger ones. Sky was not just sky to me. It was filled with magic.

"Look at all those dots dancing in the sky!" I pointed out to my schoolmates.

"Something must be wrong with your eyes. You need glasses," my friends replied in a judgmental tone.

Playing on our backyard swing set, I pretended to be riding on a rocket headed for the moon. In my four-year-old reality, I indulged in frequent trips to the moon and to an effervescent universe. On humid summer nights, my friends and I caught lightning bugs, as fireflies were called in Chicago. We put them in jars, studying them until their light burned out. Light, whether it was from the neon of Chicago's Chinatown, from Riverview Amusement Park, or from lightning bugs, mesmerized me.

One summer afternoon, as I enjoyed playing on the swings, a translucent, electric blue light appeared in front of me. An angelic being was inside. I was not afraid. This feminine presence emanated warmth and safety.

"Ricky!" she sang to me in an ethereal, high-pitched voice unlike anything I had ever heard. "There is no such thing as death. Death is nothing to fear. When you are older, many will suddenly die around you. You will be all right. There is no such thing as death." She then abruptly vanished.

Eager to share this astounding experience with my mother, I darted into the kitchen.

"Mom! There is no such thing as death. An angel just told me," I proclaimed.

"Ricky, you have such a strong imagination," my mom said, calmly continuing to prepare dinner.

Why didn't my mother and classmates believe me? Was I hallucinating or hearing things? I vowed to keep these cosmic experiences to myself. It would be safer that way. In 1982, twenty-three years later, my vision of the angel and the recollection of her message erupted in my memory as AIDS invaded my environment. Everywhere I turned, dearest friends, treasured acquaintances, and valued clients were suffering and dying from the ravages of this disease.

◆   ◆   ◆

Let me bring you back to my childhood. Sadly, at age seven, I felt like a dismal failure as a regular human being. I had a sort of dyslexia of motor and spatial coordination and could not reliably coordinate my hands. This was most obvious when I was the only kid in class who could not hold scissors correctly or catch a ball. Years later, I learned this might have been due to an injury I sustained when I was four. A student driver hit me with a car as I played in the street. My parents rushed me to the hospital. I had some stitches on my head. No big deal was made of it, but I am now convinced it threw something off in my brain chemistry and caused malcoordination.

In addition to my physical awkwardness, I had a gentleness and sensitivity that stood out. For several years, some of the more macho boys tormented me—both physically and emotionally. Underneath a façade of aloofness, I despised feeling inadequate. I constantly feared for my safety, and I was sure my imperfections would continue to cause me great misery.

Longing for approval and validation, I decided that only my special talents could redeem me. I was blessed with a crystal clear soprano voice fit for the Vienna Boys' Choir. The positive feedback I received from my relatives and teachers encouraged me to pursue an acting and singing career, starting at the age of seven. Color and light filled the theatre, and it was a safe haven for magic, secrets, and visions. The sensitivity that caused me problems at school was an asset on stage. In the Jack and Jill Players, a children's acting school in Chicago, I found acceptance. I finally felt present, seen, and heard.

My singing and acting talent was further validated when I was cast at the age of eleven in the Broadway and national touring companies of the musical *Oliver!* I did not doubt this would happen. I wanted to be in *Oliver!* more passionately than I had wanted anything before. The experience of being in that show continues to be a high point in my life. A world of possibility opened up as my mother and I traveled around the country, stayed in hotels, rode in limos, and were treated like celebrities. While I reveled in the attention, the experience of doing the show is what thrilled me. Eight shows each week, I was a pickpocket in Dickens' London. When *Oliver!* closed, I was very sad to return to Chicago and be an ordinary elementary school student again.

Fortunately, I found solace again at Jack and Jill, where every child (between the ages of four and eighteen) played a leading role at one time or another. At various times, I was the King in *The King and I*, Billy Bigelow in *Carousel*, Captain von Trapp in *The Sound of Music*, and Tevye in *Fiddler on the Roof*. My tribe of friends and budding romances were all cultivated at Jack and Jill. At one point, I even had a small national fan club listed in *Teen Screen Magazine* between the Beatles and the Rolling Stones!

However, the discrepancy between my theatrical and daily life was still a problem. It was most significant during my early high school years, when I spent evenings enthusiastically appearing in productions at Chicago's local theaters with Sam Wannamaker, Carrie Snodgrass, and Joe Mantegna. During the day, I feared for my life at school. One of the worst times was after Martin Luther King Jr.'s assassination. All hell broke loose at Bowen High. Gangs wielding knives and chains surrounded my school. Someone was shot in the lunchroom. Some boys gave me death threats. Previously, boys had tried drowning me in swim class. In the small park in front of Bowen, a very tall African American boy approached me while holding a baseball bat.

"I'm going to kill you!" he declared. His eyes burned with hatred.

A new, surprising sense of inner tranquility instantly replaced my pounding heart and sweaty palms. It was as if a presence of love and protection engulfed me, dissolving my fear. The boy looked away and quietly left. I was stunned.

This calm presence began announcing itself frequently in my offstage life. In those auspicious moments, it was as if I were bathing in unconditional love. The physical and emotional abuse ceased. Over a period of several years, I grew to feel safer and more secure on this earth.

◆   ◆   ◆

In 1972, I returned to New York City to pursue my acting and singing career. Through intense study, I grew as an actor and singer, but I also felt a counterforce leading me away from the career on which I had based my identity. While traveling around the United States with shows, fellow cast members approached me with their problems, aches, and pains. They said they felt comforted by my counseling and that their aches and pains dissolved after I sent them healing energy. My acting teacher and mentor, Jean Ramsbottom, taught me how to read tarot cards. Before long, I offered readings to friends, who said I was exceptionally gifted as a psychic.

In 1976, I moved to the then-spiritual mecca of San Francisco, where I had many profound mystical experiences. Since 1976, I have moved from coast to coast eighteen times. Some friends and family members have questioned my sanity. Others have more kindly called me a gypsy. Following my inner guidance, I was led to the perfect teachers for my spiritual development. The broad spectrum of spiritual teachings and disciplines I studied included palmistry, Actualism, Reiki, EST, the teachings of SETH, numerology, A Course in Miracles, Roman Catholicism, Ohashiatusu, Hatha Yoga, Zen Buddhism, rebirthing, primal therapy, Reichean therapy, shamanism, Siddha Yoga meditation, and Nichiren Daishonin's Buddhism. In 1985, I became an interfaith minister. Since then, I have performed several interdenominational weddings.

It has been my good fortune to be led to healers who guided me to confront and release deep-seated shame, fear, grief, and rage trapped in my body. Doing this work greatly expanded my clairvoyance and healing ability, and improved my health. I discovered intense energy coursing through my hands and body.

As I began offering sessions that combined foot reflexology, Shiatsu (Japanese acupressure), emotional healing, and clairvoyant consultations, acting jobs became scarcer. Alternatively, more people began coming to me for counseling and healings. For a while, I resisted these requests, but I gradually realized that I was called to do this work and that it brought me great joy.

My own style of working evolved into what I have named Damienwork. It is the release and transformation of physical, emotional, and psychic trauma into creative and healing energy. Just as the work itself is a synthesis of everything I have learned and experienced, Damienwork is about extracting benefit from every life experience. My practice has evolved entirely from word of mouth. After the first decade of offering healings, I had clients from New York City to Los Angeles and Hawaii, from Florida to Seattle, and in London and Paris. It has been tremendously fulfilling to see clients transform, lead workshops, and facilitate retreats.

◆   ◆   ◆

In February 2005, my father passed away after a brief illness. Grieving has led me deeper into my spiritual practices. After years of resistance, I have discovered my Karma is to be a monk in the world instead of being isolated in an ashram or monastery. In my core, I know this is my truth. While being aware of my human imperfections, I am deeply connected to my spirituality. (It's a good thing you don't have to be perfect to share your talents and observations with others!) Through the long journey of accepting my darkness and light, I have found a creative vitality that you can also attain.

I decided to write this guidebook to reach a wider audience. I can offer you my life experience and spiritual energy I have channeled into this book. Through working intensely with thousands, I have discovered strategies that can profoundly enhance the quality of your life.

Listen with your heart to what I share. You will know if something resonates for you. You will receive extra benefit if you fully participate in the contemplations and exercises in each chapter. They are designed to enable you to specifically imbibe and apply the principles discussed into your daily life in order to experience greater benefits.

I wish you great courage, fortitude, love, enlightenment and grace on your journey.

OM SHANTI OM
Richard Damien, New York City, 2005

1

Honoring Your Body as a Temple of Light

Let's begin with your body, your physical body. Some schools of spiritual thought negate the spiritual value of the physical body. These philosophies brand the physical body as disgusting, dirty, and full of sin. Devotees are trained to avoid focusing on the outer senses and their need for gratification. They must perform great austerities, such as fasting, sleep deprivation, and many hours of prayer. They are led to deny the physical body and suppress its sensual desires. In these disciplines, liberation and enlightenment will come in the next life only after denying and transcending the body. Loving the physical body is considered narcissistic and evil, worthy of punishment.

In such an atmosphere of rejection and denial of your body, how can you possibly love and respect it? I have never met anyone who truly loves and respects himself who also does not love and actively respect his physical body. A vast reservoir of riches fills your physical body in order to empower you on your spiritual path. A cellular emotional memory within your body stores your fears, shame, rejection, rage, humiliation, and abuse, as well as pleasurable and joyous experiences. Every thought, feeling, and sensation you have ever had becomes a part of you. Beginning in your mother's womb, along with physical sensations, you sense your mother's thoughts and feelings whether she is distressed, in pain, or joyously awaiting your arrival.

What role do your organs play in this?

The organs store and process both physical and emotional poisons. Visualize low-frequency cells carrying your emotional traumas through your bloodstream from organ to organ. The vibrations of these traumas feel irritating to the organs and can stimulate you to act out various compulsions instead of feeling uncomfortable sensations. For example, instead of feeling the anger in your liver, you may

1

rage at others or even create an accident to harm yourself. You might drink large quantities of alcohol and eventually contract liver disease. Remember, disease is feeling ill at ease. In this context, cirrhosis of the liver is the disease of suppressed anger manifested. If you drink lots of coffee to be in a hyperalert state instead of feeling the fear in your kidneys, your adrenals may wear down so you develop back pain. If you smoke cigarettes or marijuana instead of face sadness, your lungs could develop emphysema.

At the opposite end of the emotional spectrum, your body can carry high-frequency cells containing love and joy. These can also move from organ to organ, but they spread health and well-being. These cells become T-cells or helper cells to fight low-frequency, disease energy. If you resolve to acknowledge and feel your feelings, they will directly lead you to your spiritual nature.

Where and what is my spiritual nature?

While your body apparently stores your emotional traumas, perhaps it is less evident that a nonphysical energy exists within everyone and everything. This invisible force is your connection to your spiritual nature. Pioneer body/mind therapist Wilhelm Reich named this invisible force *orgone*. In India, this energy is known as *Prana* or *Shakti*. Chinese medicine calls it *Chi*. Japanese medicine refers to it as *ki*. This energy flows through invisible lines along your body called meridians. These meridians run everywhere, along your face, arms, torso, abdomen, legs, feet, back, head, and so forth. When you die, this life force energy leaves your body and no longer courses along the meridians. In shamanic terms, the spirit has left the body.

You may delight in experiencing your spiritual energy while making love, meditating, or receiving bodywork or acupuncture. Delicious streams of energy may flood through your meridians. When this energy flows freely, you experience pleasure and vitality. If this energy is trapped in one or more areas, you feel pain and discomfort.

It is most beneficial to adopt the concept that your spiritual nature exists within your body. In Buddhism, this is called your *Buddha Nature*. This part of you is whole and complete and lacks nothing. If unconditional love lives inside your body, wouldn't you want to treat it with respect? It is equally beneficial to respect the spiritual or Divine Nature residing in all people, animals, and aspects of nature. The Yogis say consciousness is in everything, that is, God is within everyone and everything.

If you detest your body, you may find it difficult to contemplate your inner spiritual nature. Instead, you might obsess about your physical imperfections, but constantly finding fault with your physical appearance sets the stage for future suffering. Is this what you really desire?

At the age of nineteen, I began losing my hair. I felt devastated because I feared no one would love me or receive my love if I was balding. In those days, young men did not shave their heads. Baldness was something people made fun of.

"How could I be a young, bald star?" I worried. It seemed hopeless.

Ironically, as a young adolescent, I hated my hair. It was wavy and unruly, and winglike flips emerged from the sides when it grew longer. For a brief period, I even pulled out hair on the top of my head, completely unaware of the distress I would feel when it began falling out on its own later! At the age of fifty, I decided to get a hairpiece for a year as I put myself out as an actor and singer in New York City. It looked great, very natural. I wanted to experience having hair for a year, and I did! I accept myself with and without hair. In my experience, most people obsess about physical imperfections at one time or another. Yet when they accept their bodies as they are, they invite greater happiness into their lives.

Aren't I entitled to my preferences?

Of course you are. Accepting your body as it is does not mean you are not entitled to your preferences. A man may desire more hair, a well-toned abdomen, and a larger penis. A woman may prefer larger (or smaller) breasts or hips. You may desire a very high standard of beauty for yourself. I have sometimes laughed at my desire to become my version of a perfect male specimen, even though I know I will never look like Brad Pitt. Humans may feel that becoming a perfect Adonis or Venus will bring them closer to divine status and will grant immortality, but, of course, this is just wishful thinking.

Once you have had the profound experience of your inner light and unconditional love, it is easier and more soothing to accept your body as it is. You may choose to make external changes knowing they will not bring you joy and inner peace. Outer changes do not dispel any core feelings of inadequacy, as I have witnessed with several clients.

I have known people who had a great deal of plastic surgery on their faces and bodies. Even though they may seem more confident, they have lost the beautiful spark of life and uniqueness. They seem duller and less radiant. They sometimes look odd, as if they have lost a part of their soul. Maybe they have. Internally, they must still deal with their core issues. Sometimes, new problems arise, requiring expensive visits for repair and maintenance work, both physical and emotional.

When you reject your body, this is transmitted to others. It is as if you have a subtle radar saying, "I hate my body…I can't stand my big nose…I hate my bald spot." Subliminally, others react and sense these messages, ironically attracting just the sort of attention you do not want. Accepting your body right now (fat, thin, tall, flabby, pockmarked, and so forth) is where you must begin.

Being Grounded

Once you choose to accept your body, another question arises. Are you willing to be fully here on this earth, to show up fully in your life?

During my Damienwork sessions, as I scan a client's energy field, I am sometimes surprised to see how many people are not grounded or connected to the earth. Some of us literally do not experience our feet on the ground. As a result, we may:

- Be accident-prone.

- Often feel drained or exhausted. Some are diagnosed with Epstein-Barr virus (EBV) or Chronic Fatigue Syndrome (CFS).

- Easily be thrown off balance if life does not fit our expectations.

- Be constantly disappointed, leading to frequent bouts of depression.

- Procrastinate often, feeling it's never the right time to move ahead. "I'm too busy…I'm pooped…I just never have the time!"

- Not finish what we start, always moving on to something new. "I'm bored…It's just too difficult…I need to give myself more pleasure in life!"

- Feel lost and isolated, suffering from what shamans call "soul loss" or losing parts of your essence.

How can you feel grounded in a bustling city like New York City or London?

While initially living in New York City, the land of concrete, it was difficult to feel very connected to Mother Earth. I relished in excursions to magnificent Central Park or the majestic Cloisters in Fort Tryon at the northern tip of the island. When I regularly imagine sending roots (yes, like tree roots) from my body deep into the earth, a sensation of nurturance occurs. My thinking slows down, and I am better able to face life's challenges, including the thousands of tourists outside my door.

I did not even begin to feel grounded until my late twenties, and it has been an ongoing process of deepening my relationship with nature. When I do feel grounded, it is easier to see more beauty in people and nature. In this state, taking a walk invokes an intensification of light and color similar to my childhood experiences. It can be quite spectacular. When I am in a city like Manhattan, I particularly appreciate the surprising patches of nature around me. They soothe and inspire me. Daily, I silently offer thanks for this beauty.

Grounding Exercise

Imagine roots from your tailbone grow down to the molten core of the earth. Feel Mother Earth supporting you with her nurturing presence. Be here now. Take a short walk outdoors while consciously breathing and being present with nature. Slow down your thinking. Focus on your breath with ease. Notice beauty around you, even if you live in a run-down neighborhood. Around the next corner, a striking purple door or patch of sunflowers may greet you. If you are willing to see them, surprises await you everywhere.

Exercise and Breath

If you are not breathing deeply, it is very difficult to feel your presence in your body. The breath connects us directly to the body and its energy meridians. Observe how there is a slight tingling movement of energy throughout your energy meridians when you are relaxed. Your body is breathing itself.

We are a nation of hypra-ventilators (that is, shallow breathers). For some of us, the only time we take a deep breath is when we smoke or during a medical exam. Many of us barely breathe while having sex. Yet, breath fuels your delicious sensations and increases your sexual stamina.

Pay attention to how often you hold your breath. Are you breathing now? Oxygenate your blood right now with a nice, slow, deep breath.

Exercising is a great way to consciously enjoy breathing. Listen to your body to find what exercise program works best for you. Is it biking, walking, hiking, running, dancing, yoga, martial arts, sports, kickboxing, aerobics, weight training, or Pilates?

Find ways to breathe more deeply. One reason I enjoy singing so much is that it is literally a breathing workout. Not only does the power of the breath create amazing sounds, it is physically revitalizing.

Breathing Exercise

The simple practice of conscious breathing can help you reduce stress, anxiety, and confusion in your life. Breathing consciously for a few minutes can get you out of your head and into the abundant life force energy in your body. Your breath is a profound vehicle linking you to your spirit.

Right now, take ten long, full breaths, connecting the inhale and the exhale. Do not pause between breaths. You may keep your mouth either closed or open during the entire cycle. Allow the breath to flow like a circle, continually renewing itself. You might feel your body tingling. Enjoy it.

In 1984, I was rebirthed, the process of reliving and releasing birth trauma. Deep, connected breathing is the major vehicle in this work. It was agonizing to sustain deep breathing for two or three hours at a time. Wet rebirthing, done with a snorkel while fully immersed underwater, was especially challenging. However, the pain eventually shifted to exquisite relaxation. My body hummed as it fully breathed on its own, effortlessly and graciously.

Since that time, when I experience fear or anxiety, my body begins breathing deeply on its own or I yawn. Yawning is the body's natural way of relaxing and taking in more oxygen. How comforting it can be to experience my breath joining me to my spirit.

Diet and Purification

Every human being has a different chemical structure, so it is ridiculous to pontificate about what is right or wrong for everyone to eat. I am convinced your blood type, metabolic type, body type, and genetics greatly influence your health, powers of elimination, and assimilation.

Some Chinese acupuncturists startled me when they suggested I regularly eat pork and lamb. However, when I followed their advice, I felt revitalized. For years, I resisted these meats, believing they were harmful and definitely not spiritual.

Isn't vegetarianism the diet of peace?

One nutritionist suggested I become a vegetarian. I tried this for a while and became quite thin. I continued trying to convince myself that this was the most spiritual diet because Gandhi had said so and it would rapidly lead me to enlightenment. However, when I learned Adolf Hitler and the most violent tribe in Africa were all strict vegetarians, I questioned the inherent spirituality of this or any diet. Although some people have received enormous health benefits from vegetarianism and macrobiotics, others I have known are quite sickly. Obsessed with eating the right, pure foods and fearful of eating supposedly impure foods, they punish themselves if they slip off the diet.

You can take responsibility for your health by listening to your body and finding which foods are most beneficial for you. Periodically, your diet and eating habits may change as part of the ongoing process of inner listening. We often crave foods to which we are most allergic. It is useful to periodically stop eating such foods. For a three-month period several years ago, I avoided the foods I was allergic to. Under the guidance of a nutritionist, I embarked on a cleansing regime with herbs, vitamins, and supplements. My allergies subsided, and my body felt reenergized.

Detoxifying and abstaining are ways to honor your body, helping you distinguish between your true inner voice and the voice of your addictions.

Purification is necessary as the next step of self-healing. Massage, acupuncture, chiropractic adjustments (I especially recommend NUCA-upper cervical adjustments, which very subtly, without much force or velocity, adjust your occiput/brain stem, causing your entire spine to come into alignment), herbs, homeopathy, naturopathy, and colonics help purify the body of accumulated toxins. If not expelled, layers of poisons remain submerged in your liver, gall bladder, and intestines. With the assistance of a well-informed health professional, you can participate in a customized cleansing program. Once you have shed a great deal of your accumulated toxins, it will be easier and safer to inwardly know which foods are truly beneficial for you. Otherwise, you may continue craving and eating the very foods that weaken your system.

Eating organic foods helps you accumulate fewer toxins to begin with. Sodas and products containing artificial sweeteners can weaken your immune system, sometimes leading to fibromyalgia. You may need to make a solid commitment to eating foods that are beneficial instead of merely pleasurable.

Have you ever directed healing energy into your food and liquids? From Native American and Yogic teachings, I have learned that blessing your food is a way of respecting life. Everything in this world is interconnected. Food comes to us from the earth and eventually returns to the earth. In monasteries, abbeys, and ashrams all over the world, the meals are blessed. The nuns and monks then eat their meals in silence. Blessing your food is a reminder that you are part of something greater that sustains you.

Blessing Your Food Exercise

1. Place both hands over food you are about to eat. From your heart, send gratitude for the sacrifice the animals, fruits, vegetables, legumes, and grains have made for your benefit.

2. Imagine that healing energy from the universe is flowing through your hands, purifying and revitalizing the food for you.

3. Eat your food in silence. Be conscious of what you are eating. Savor the flavor. Chew consciously. Take your time.

Rest

It is surprising how my friends, family, and clients can so easily forget a basic rule. Your physical body requires frequent rest periods. Have you ever noticed others straining to fill their lives with twelve or more hours a day of nonstop activity? Rushing from engagement to commitment to appointment, these folks are often tardy and just worn-out.

Some of us avidly schedule several hours of a high-impact exercise program, but we fail to schedule downtime for our muscles to assimilate those workouts. Honoring your body as a temple of light includes allotting frequent rest periods. Do you remember rest periods in school? Those breaks were always rejuvenating for me. Now, when my body feels exhausted from fulfilling my travel commitments, I give myself a day to regroup. I schedule a massage, acupuncture treatment, or NUCA-upper cervical adjustment to align and renew my energy.

My private practice includes doing intense healing work in order to release trauma from surgeries, accidents, toxins from drugs, as well as physical and sexual abuse. To be of service, I must renew myself first. On days when I feel my work takes too much out of me I will nap, do extra chanting or meditation, and practice silence. Silence brings rest to the tongue, body, and mind. Silence renews your energy and is a form of rest. Nuns and monks practice silence during retreats or certain periods of the day. I find this very revitalizing, so I am not available to others at certain times.

At times, I require less sleep and feel I am in an exalted state. The cycles of our physical stamina vary. More rest and sleep may be necessary when dealing with crises and life challenges. It is okay to rest. After my father's death, I experienced what is sometimes called death fatigue. I only wanted to sleep and be alone. I had to claim periods of time when I was sleeping, resting, and processing. I sometimes felt guilty that I was not working and being there for friends, but I feel greatly renewed and more courageous because of this period.

Know you do not always have to be productive. Honoring your body as a temple is a spiritual practice. Being grounded, accepting your body as it is today, exercising, practicing deep breathing, following an appropriate diet, practicing purification, silence, and resting are the necessary guidelines.

Honoring Your Body as a Temple of Light: Experiential Exercise

1. Take off all your clothing, and stand in front of a mirror.

2. Take several deep, yet gentle, breaths as you scan your body in the mirror. Observe the front, back, and sides of your body. Give yourself permission to be present with your reflection.

3. Recall any parts of your body you have rejected. How did you express your rejection? What was your behavior? Did you hide or abuse those body parts? Did you send hateful thoughts to your body?

4. Are you having difficulty accepting any body parts today? How are you dealing with this? How would it feel to change those judgments and behaviors? Take a moment now to forgive yourself for harming or rejecting your body. Look into your eyes, and tell yourself that you forgive yourself right now.

5. As you gaze into your reflection, envision your body encasing your spiritual essence. Your body is indeed sacred. Affirm these things three times aloud, "I honor you, my body, my temple. My Buddha Nature (or God or higher power) lives inside of you. Teach me to love, nurture, and respect you moment by moment."

6. Starting at the crown of your head and then moving down to your toes, send an inner smile to yourself from the inside out. Take your time while enjoying this exercise. It is very good for your immune system and can help lift depression from your cells.

You have just begun to honor your body as a temple of light. You can do the inner smile anytime and anywhere. It is a fabulous immune booster.

Honoring Your Body as a Temple of Light: Written Contemplation

Consider the following questions, and write your observations. Be sure to speak lovingly to yourself.

1. Have you ever experienced a spiritual power or essence in your body? If so, when?

2. Do you tend to feel grounded and present in your body? Do you often live in your head? Are you accident-prone? Do you feel depleted? Do you ever feel like you have lost a part of your essence?

3. What feels like the appropriate exercise program for your body? What would this program look like?

4. Do you take several deep breaths regularly? Are you conscious of your breathing? If so, when?

5. Which foods and beverages are not serving your body? Are you willing to replace them with more nutritious foods? What are those foods? Do you drink enough pure water? Do you eat too little or too much?

6. Are you sleeping enough or getting enough rest? Do you ever practice silence? Do you take naps? Do you listen to your body and give it the rest it craves?

Your connection to your spiritual nature is right there in your body.

2

Honoring Your Emotions as Allies

What are our emotions anyway?

Emotions are "feelings in motion," sensations literally moving through your body. These feelings and sensations move through your organs, eliciting different responses at different times. When you see your child or your team wins the World Series, you may feel as if your heart is pounding with joy. When you feel frightened, your throat may be parched and tight, or your teeth may chatter. When you are angry, your head may feel on fire.

Throughout the ages, spiritual seekers have complained about the seemingly endless array of obstacles they have encountered on the spiritual path. Seekers pray these obstacles will dissolve quickly so that everything can flow smoothly. Perhaps the greatest hindrance seekers have faced is the sometimes overwhelming power of their own emotions. After a long, dry period, a seeker may suddenly have the good fortune to experience a profound opening. He or she may feel as if ominous, oppressive black clouds have parted and a golden sun is finally shining. Everything feels illuminated at that moment.

These glowing experiences encourage you to persevere, yet they are not lasting. They are just a taste of the state of Buddhahood and unconditional love. Through your efforts on the spiritual path, you can reside more and more frequently in that state. Everything in this book is chosen to create openings so you may have these radiant experiences. You were born to have these experiences as you live in the thick of the world.

Have you ever noticed a rush of so-called negative emotions often follow blissful, high states? Someone irritates you; you experience anger. Not enough money is in your bank account to pay your bills; you experience fear. After such happiness and joy, when these downer emotions arise, the seeker wails, "Why is this happening to me? What did I do wrong?"

First, you must understand the potential for all the levels of consciousness and all emotional states exists within you at any moment. You could live in a sumptuous palace surrounded by the most delicious food. You could own the most exquisite art and wear the most comfortable, beautiful silk clothing. Yet, inwardly, you could be in the most miserable state of hell. Alternatively, you could be living as Mother Theresa did, serving the poorest of the poor in the slums of Calcutta. Yet, you could be in a state of bliss from alleviating suffering with enormous compassion.

As you sustain a higher, more serene state for longer periods, you will still have to deal with the accompanying emotions. They do not vanish when you become enlightened. Instead, you have a different experience of them. They move rapidly through your body, and you let go of them quickly. Do not worry. Nothing is wrong. In fact, everything is working perfectly, my friends.

The Context of Purification

Let's begin to view our emotions in a different context. Instead of seeing emotions as a hindrance, it is possible to reap great benefit from all of your emotional states. Emotions can help purify you and help you release baggage from the past, bringing you more fully into an enhanced awareness of the now.

If you are to embody love, compassion, and wisdom more fully in your life, your vessel needs to be pure. In order to create a pure vessel, you must release and transmute your emotions. Day-to-day living can easily trigger your latent past impressions of loss, abandonment, and humiliation. Lust, hunger, and greed—as well as all your happy past impressions—may become reactivated as well. During each moment, you have the choice to act out an uncomfortable emotion in a negative way (for example, yelling at a coworker out of irritation or cheating on your partner out of vindictiveness) or consciously breathe and feel the energy of the emotion as it passes through your body. Emotions are never bad or wrong. They are merely energy. They are the perfect vehicle for your purification and transformation moment by moment. Trust in this process. Now, let's examine emotions more closely.

Fear

Imagine the planets vibrating throughout the universe are also inside your body, influencing your emotions. In Greek mythology, Pluto is the lord of the underworld. The planet Pluto rules the emotion of fear. Plutonian feelings run very deep. Pluto represents your most primal subconscious fears. These disturbing fears sometimes emerge unexpectedly when things are apparently going well. You may experience profound intimacy in a relationship and suddenly find yourself obsessing about the possibility of losing it. For example, you might fear that you may be rejected or abandoned. You might fear that your beloved may die and so forth.

In Oriental medicine, the kidney and the bladder meridians rule fear. It is interesting to note that, when we are afraid, there is often an instinctual urge to urinate. The wisdom in your body wants to support you in releasing your fear. Pluto rules the subterranean tunnels of the subconscious, where core fears lurk:

- The Fear of Abandonment: Being alone, unloved, and unseen

- The Fear of Humiliation and Rejection: Overt and covert criticisms that sting

- The Fear of Abuse: Physical and/or psychological violence

If you breathe and follow these fears to their depths, you will discover your most primal fear, the fear of death. Sinking into the fear of death is like entering a black hole. There is nothing in this space. Many resist ever visiting this space.

I have often guided clients into that void. Initially, some were very anxious about lingering there. Eventually, they discovered it was possible to surrender and experience great peace and tranquility. Their reality shifted from resistance to serene acceptance. Their faces relaxed, and their breathing became very even.

Entering the void and following your fears to their core, you can experience a transmutation of your fear. The next time you feel emptiness, instead of avoiding it, you can quietly breathe into it, deeply sinking into it and realize hidden peace and quiet.

Honoring fear, you may experience more tingling and vibration as the fear moves through your body. Instead of contracting, you might experience a shaking or slight trembling. No, you are not having a breakdown. You are having a breakthrough! The fear is being released and transmuted. Experiencing fear is nothing to fear. We will explore this more deeply in chapter 3.

Moodiness

Instead of being a specific emotion, moodiness encompasses all of the emotions. The ruling planet for moodiness is the moon, which passes through a new astrological sign every two or two-and-a-half days. Our fastest moving planet, it greatly influences the ebb and flow of ocean tides as well as both the water and body temperature of humans. In Indian or Vedic astrology, the moon is considered the most powerful influence on the state of our minds. In Western or tropical astrology, the moon purportedly rules our emotions. The stomach is the organ the moon rules. Even though that may seem remote from emotions, the moon is classically seen as being female. Thus, it is a source of nourishment. Representing the mother, or nurturing aspect of the universe, the moon rules the astrological sign of Cancer. You may either use the positive energy of the moon to nurture yourself and others with delicious, easily digestible, nutritious foods or find other opportunities for nurturance.

Is there a value in moodiness?

Yes, moodiness provides us with an impetus for the awareness of our inner state amidst the often-chaotic changes of the world. We are not static beings. We live in an ever-changing universe, so it is natural and useful to experience gradations of feeling and desire. The changes inherent in moodiness enable you to be more aware of your experience. During one moment, you may desire sexual contact. The next, you may want a nap. You may find yourself feeling very irritable for a while. Sadness or melancholy may then follow. The next minute, you might be ecstatic about being asked on a date. You can witness your moods and desires without needing to act them all out or talk about them. Just because you desire a chocolate bar does not mean you must have one. You have a choice. Alan Watts, the late, great spiritual author, referred to our thoughts, feelings, and desires as clouds passing on the screen of our conscious awareness.

Clouds Passing Exercise

For five minutes, close your eyes. Witness your thoughts, feelings, and desires. Breathe consciously while staying present in your body. Imagine all you witness as clouds passing on a vast, blue sky. Just observe. Do nothing about these thoughts, feelings, and desires. What happened to them?

Anger

In Oriental medicine, the liver rules anger. Too much anger can stress the energy of the liver, decreasing your life force. In astrology, Mars is the designated planet of anger with its fiery red countenance. Most of us have been red-faced in the throes of anger at one time or another.

It is too easy to dismiss anger as a solely negative emotion. After all, haven't you witnessed anger wreak havoc in your relationships? This is the malevolent aspect of anger. It lashes out, dumping poison on others. It can be deeply toxic to the angry person as well. There may be a lack of concern for the feeling of others as anger parades as selfishness. The focus becomes "Me, me, me!" A person teeming with rage wants to unload this terribly uncomfortable feeling as quickly as possible.

Each emotion does have value for your spiritual growth. As with fear, there is a positive aspect to anger. Fiery Mars rules Aries, the first astrological sign, whose motto is, "I am." Anger enables each of us, regardless of our astrological sign, to affirm, "I am. I am here. I am alive. I deserve to be treated with respect!"

Saying "I am" affirms your existence. You are not a victim in life. Regardless of what your circumstances are or have been, you can use the positive aspect of anger to choose not to live as a victim. It is an act of self-love and personal power to declare, "I am not a victim. I am not going to allow anyone to abuse me physically, sexually, emotionally, or psychically. I may have been a victim before, but no more!"

As for me, it took a great deal of feeling victimized before I could say, "Enough already! I am! I am a worthy person. I am a being of light." My anger has motivated me to stop allowing myself to remain in situations where I feel victimized. When the pain of abuse became intolerable, I began taking responsibility for my own well-being instead of waiting for outer circumstances to shift. I removed myself from negative people in my life.

Anger is not only overt, as in yelling or raging. It can be hiding in subtle manifestations such as frustration, bitterness, criticism, pessimism, gossiping, hopelessness, jealousy, irritation, scarcity, sarcasm, and even loneliness. But anger can also motivate you to move forward with a positive vitality. It can loosen the chains of rigidity and become a strong catalyst for movement in your life. Saying no to an abusive relationship and moving on may empower you to create new realities in your life. For example, leaving an abusive boss can inspire you to finally enroll in that class and begin creating the career you most desire."

When I have examined my anger or the anger of others, I have always found fear lurking underneath. Often, it is the fear of not having your desires fulfilled or, on a deeper level, primal fears of abandonment, humiliation, rejection, or abuse. By acknowledging the hidden fears beneath your anger, you can breathe and move the upset through your body. The anger will dissolve into fear and then into life force energy.

The Kapalabhati breath in yoga, or "breath of fire," is fast, deep, rhythmic abdominal breathing done through the nostrils. This is a great technique for moving anger through your body and dispersing it. While practicing Kapalabhati breathing, I visualize sending my anger to a benevolent dragon who is consuming it. As a result, I feel greatly energized, more alert, and aware. Using a punching bag is also quite effective. If you don't have a punching bag, kick your mattress. As you pound and scream into your pillow, shout, "No! I won't let you do this! I am not a victim!"

These techniques help dissipate and transmute the mighty energy of anger. The energy in anger can move mountains. The new vitality acquired can be used to create positive change. I have witnessed this energy in those who became leading activists in the fight for women's rights, civil rights, and gay rights. It is as if this anger at the stance of victimhood motivates people to work long hours passionately, becoming agents for change. For some, expressing anger is easy. Others indulge their anger by having very public, dramatic tantrums. While the individual may benefit somewhat from the emotional release, this never transforms anger into something positive. The person is merely indulging without consciously respecting the power of anger. He or she is oblivious to dumping poison on others. For this reason, I recommend having private temper tantrums!

On the other hand, suppressed anger can create illness and disease, literally eating away at your body, so let's find ways to transform anger that support our health and environment.

Transforming Anger Exercise

When experiencing anger, ask yourself:

1. Who (or what) do I feel is threatening or victimizing me?

2. What am I afraid will happen?

3. What do I fear I will lose here? Breathe. Send that fear through your body.

4. When you feel calm, ask the most beneficial, appropriate action to take be revealed to you.

5.   Listen to your inner voice, or write in your journal. Take your time. The answer will arrive.

Depression

The planet Saturn, or the taskmaster, the disciplinarian of the cosmos, represents a restrictive, depressed emotional state. Through discipline, which is Saturn's positive aspect, you can work through your Karmic obstacles and lessons. You persevere and receive great benefits. When moving through such a restrictive period, you must continue to take great care of yourself because your positive actions will attract positive support. Eventually, you will triumph over your circumstances. Discipline creates consistency and, eventually, inner freedom.

Depression, Saturn's negative aspect, may be viewed as a great resistance to change. We do not want to accept what has transpired while we struggle to hold on to past jobs, home, family, relationships, or dreams of what could have been. Obviously, I am not addressing the condition that medical doctors diagnose as purely chemical depression. This kind of depression exists. Yet, from my own experience with thousands of people, I have seen there is always an element of resistance to letting go and accepting what is whenever there is depression.

Have you ever noticed you breathe shallowly when you feel depressed? Underneath depression are a host of feelings such as anger, fear, and loss. A part of you does not want to experience these feelings and becomes stuck. Breathing deeply connects us more fully to our grief and loss. We may cry, and our jaws may quiver, but, once we can grieve our losses, the depression begins to release, dissolving into a state of hopefulness.

Depression does not need to threaten your life. Many people have come to me depressed because they have lost a parent, mate, or, sometimes, a pet. Through this experience, they have lost a part of their soul. As they move through the grieving process, with the assistance of my spirit animals on the other, nonphysical realms, I draw back soul parts that were lost due to shock and grief. Experiencing soul loss is a very human occurrence. Once my clients are able to grieve fully and accept what happened, many soul parts return to them. They then emerge more courageously in their lives.

The lungs represent grief in Oriental medicine. The benefit of grieving is that it can lead you to accept the impermanence of this temporal world. Accepting the nature of life, you are free to choose different responses to loss. Depression can be an opportunity to see how deep your consciousness lies. When you are led to the death space, you can emerge revivified. Some of the most joyous days of my life have followed my deepest depression. Through grieving for my acting career and social life, I could hear my inner voice guiding me to become a healer, writer, and teacher.

Joy

Joy is the state where we easily accept our inner state or outer circumstances. When there is joy, there is no resistance. There is a buoyant state of well-being, an expanded sense of loving life.

I hope that you will experience love and acceptance thousands upon thousands of times in your life. Love is acceptance, and acceptance welcomes joy. This is why I am not focusing on love as an emotion. Experiencing joy brings you fully into the now. Joy emerges from deep within, like a refreshing, soothing inner breeze. You can also experience joy spontaneously by being in the presence of a truly loving being, listening to music, viewing a work of art, creating something, or taking in the majesty of nature. Some of my most joyful moments have occurred unexpectedly, for example, observing the beauty in people waiting in line at the supermarket, noticing the holiness in my mother as she set the dining room table, or having a friendly dog or cat visit.

The ruling planet of joy is the Sun. In the traditional Rider Tarot deck, the Sun card reveals a joyous infant/inner child illuminated by a brilliant sun. The greater your capacity for experiencing joy, the more frequently you will feel a higher state of consciousness and bliss. These expansive, sometimes ecstatic states are a reward for riding through the challenges of fear, anger, and loss that life guarantees us.

Honoring Your Emotions as Allies: Experiential Exercise

1. Imagine the entire universe of planets, stars, and galaxies live inside your body.

2. Place your hands over your kidneys in your lower back. Honor the presence of fear in your kidneys and bladder. Notice what you are presently afraid of in your life. Breathe deeply, sending the energy of fear into your kidneys and bladder. Conjure up the presence of Pluto, the lord of the underworld. Imagine he lives in your kidneys and bladder. Ask yourself, "How does fear stop me in my life? What would it feel like to have the courage to move

through my fears?" Envision Pluto helping you move through your fears, facing them, so you keep moving forward. See yourself sharing your talents with others, contributing more fully to your community. Visualize yourself transcending your fears and experiencing victory over them. Send an inner smile into your kidneys and adrenals.

3. Place your hands over your stomach on the left side under your ribs. Conjure up the presence of the moon. Notice how your thoughts, desires, and emotions are constantly changing. Visualize yourself on a surfboard riding your many moods like waves, being aware of them with appropriate flexibility. Enjoy your accomplishment as you return to shore and step off your surfboard.

4. Place your hands over your liver on your right side under your ribs. Imagine your liver is glowing with red light. Invoke the presence of Mars in your liver. What do you have anger about? Affirm, "I am not a victim! I will not let this destroy my happiness!" Visualize your anger giving you the courage to take positive actions in your life. See yourself as being courageously compassionate.

5. You have the power to transmute anger with your breath. Practice Kapalabhati breathing from your abdomen. Close your mouth, breathing through your nostrils. Firmly contract your abdomen to exhale. As you automatically inhale, let your abdomen expand. Do this rhythmically. As it becomes familiar and comfortable, speed up the pace. It will sound like panting. Do three groups of nine Kapalabhati breaths at a time. Get a sense of what it feels like to not be victimized by anger. Send an inner smile to your liver.

6. Place one hand over each lung. Conjure up the planet Saturn living in your lungs. What are you grieving about? What (or who) do you need to release? Send an inner smile to your lungs.

7. Place both hands over your heart. Recall some experiences when you felt joyful. Where were you? What was happening in your environment? What was happening inside you? Feel those feelings again. Imagine a golden sun inside your heart, beaming out through your entire body. Celebrate the power of joy. Give yourself permission to sink deeper into your joy. Send an inner smile deep into your heart.

As you sustain a higher, more serene state for longer periods, you will still have to deal with your accompanying emotions. Nothing is wrong. Everything is working perfectly. Emotions are feelings in motion. It is possible to reap great benefits from all of your emotional states. Emotions can help purify you and help you release baggage from the past, bringing you more fully into the celebration of the now.

3

Transforming Fear into Creativity

What is this mysterious power over our lives called fear? Is it a force, emotion, curse, or secret blessing? As a male raised in the American culture of the 1950s and 1960s, teachers often reprimanded my fellow students and me if we expressed our fear.

"Are you girls scared? Do you want mommy?" my physical education instructor bellowed before a class of nude teenage boys about to dive into a frigid, highly chlorinated swimming pool. Whenever a fellow student in gym class expressed his fear or dared cry, a humiliating attack followed. "Sissy! You are such a girl!"

How was I to endure this shaming in my high school environment and yet honor my sensitivity? I found myself tightening my chest, holding my breath, swallowing the fear, and generally numbing myself. Who wants to endure that kind of shaming? I did not understand that all of that fear would become trapped in my body and I could not escape it at all.

Is it safe to admit with your loved ones when you are afraid of certain people, events, or things? Sharing your fears with those around you may be met with, "Don't be afraid. Everything will be okay." Of course, our friends and loved ones do not want to see us suffer. That's okay. If I share my fears, I know I would rather people acknowledge hearing me instead of trying to convince me to remove the fear. Ideally, a safe, supportive environment (therapy or counseling) needs to be created in order to fully share our fears. Many of us are uncomfortable dealing with fear, whether it is fear of others or ourselves.

Can we ever be completely free of fear?

Probably not. However, the opportunity does exist to transform fear into creativity through your thoughts, words, and actions. You can find new responses to deal with the fears permeating your life. Eradicating fear completely is not desirable, as you will soon discover. Believe it or not, there are even some positive aspects to fear.

What could be positive about fear?

Programmed into our nervous systems is a fight-or-flight mechanism, a primal impulse to trust instinct in the presence of possible danger. This instinct protects you. For example, as a pedestrian crossing an intersection, you must react appropriately if a car is rapidly approaching and there may not be enough time to think logically about what to do. The fight-or-flight instinct causes you to see danger and leap to safety almost simultaneously. This is just one example of how your fear can save your life and/or the lives of others.

What does Karma have to do with fear?

Understanding how the law of cause and effect in the universe, or Karma, works, you can live more consciously and more mindfully. (See chapter 8.) Then you can discover how your thoughts, words, and actions create and influence both your inner reality and outer environment. Choosing to change your Karma to experience greater harmony, you become more mindful of never deliberately harming yourself and others, including animals and our beloved planet. The fear of repercussions from harmful deeds can be enough to prevent you from performing them. Fear can support you in being aware of the consequences, or Karma, of your actions.

What happens when you suppress fear?

As discussed in chapter 1, suppressed emotions lie within your tissues, organs, and cells. Suppressed or inexperienced fear becomes a permanent part of your chemistry. Extreme suppression of fear takes the form of compulsive behavior that can lead to illness and disease. For example, instead of acknowledging and feeling your fears, you might overspend, overtalk, overeat, overdrink, overcaffeinate, or oversex to stuff down your anxiety.

Suppressing fear creates a vicious cycle that actually creates more fear. When you avoid facing your fears, the situation or person you are avoiding will assume gigantic proportions in your imagination.

As an awkward, skinny high school student, I dreaded physical education class, where the other boys often taunted and tormented me. I felt nauseous at breakfast every morning. Great energy was invested in praying that auditions or acting jobs would provide a much-needed escape. This fear of physical and emotional abuse persisted for months. Things did not improve until my parents relocated to a new neighborhood and I joined a new school. Only then, I realized how much energy I had been investing in being a victim for my tormentors. I discovered the fear fueled my abusers, causing the drama to persist.

At my new school, I made a point of actually playing basketball instead of sweating it out in the bleachers as I had felt compelled to do for years. I was amazed; despite playing poorly, I never experienced shame or abuse. This new reality left me giddy with happiness for the remaining eighteen months of high school. When I discovered that continuing to resist the situation was more painful than actually participating in sports, my fear transformed into courage and greater self-esteem. It was the first time, apart from my performing career, I experienced my personal power.

What is creativity? How can fear become creativity?

Creativity is the freedom to respond with different choices to the circumstances life presents, instead of acting like an automaton and having only one response to an upsetting situation (for example, yelling, crying, pouting, struggling, leaving, sabotaging opportunity, or playing the victim). You have the freedom to choose how you respond. You can pause, breathe deeply, and contemplate your appropriate response a relaxed manner. Just as actors, singers, musicians, painters, and writers make choices to endow their work with brilliance, the choices you make in life are the essence of your creativity.

Since childhood, I have had an intimate relationship with fear of performing and auditioning. Before going onstage, I often experienced butterflies in my stomach. As my throat began closing down, I would begin to yawn and relax. Venturing onstage, I would utilize my fear as fuel for a more heightened state. As a result, my performance was more alive and spontaneous. This is using fear as creative energy.

In 1996, I decided to perform my cabaret act in Manhattan for the first time in fifteen years. Before the show began, I heard a persistent inner thought, "You don't want to go on. Cancel the show." Because of this thought, I literally began the show on the wrong note. Instead of losing my composure, I chose to be present with the fear, which was masquerading as dread. To my delight, I experienced a very organic, though quite challenging, performance. Deeply connected to the audience, my defenses were down. I transformed my fear into creativity. If you move forward with it, the energy of the fear becomes exciting and revitalizing.

We have all experienced fear of the unknown. Instead of paralyzing you, this fear can provide the energy you need to explore new territory and find venues for self-expression.

Is it possible to make peace with fear?

This would be a different world if we could make friends with our fears. It is as if the universe has designed fear for us to deepen our spiritual journey. It will always be with you in one form or another. Every time you experience fear as energy moves through your body, instead of an obstacle, you can move forward and cultivate greater courage. Each time you succeed at this, it is as if you are programming a new response to recall next time. With this practice, fear is easier to tolerate and transform into useful energy.

Models

Great humanitarians, spiritual leaders, and masters in the arts nourish us with the inspiration of their example. It is desirable to have models who motivate and inspire you, courageous people who have remained true to their principles and vision despite great hardship, persecution, or abuse. These people have moved through their fears to fulfill a higher vision for humanity.

Vanessa Redgrave, the astoundingly talented actress, has taken some political positions that have caused her to lose acting work, yet she continues to be dedicated to serving humanity. Despite being misunderstood, she pursues a brilliant acting career. I had the honor of meeting her once in London, when she was playing Arkadina in *The Seagull*. She was so present and radiant that she had an obviously positive effect on everyone around her, including the stage doorman and waiting fans. Maya Angelou, the poet, writer, actress, dancer, director and activist, endured sexual abuse as a child and stopped speaking, yet she understood "Why the Caged Bird Sings" and transformed the suffering through her creative voice.

Martin Luther King Jr. and Mahatma Gandhi have also inspired me. Their courage, compassion, and commitment to a higher vision for humanity make them embodiments of courage in action. When you fully focus on someone who is courageously compassionate, it reanimates those qualities inside of you. As a result, you will experience your own courage and greater equanimity. This is known as focusing on a form (role model) to find the formless (his or her essence) within ourselves.

Role Model Exercise

Think of someone—alive or dead—who has expressed great courage. Imagine he or she is sitting across from you, holding your hands. Consciously breathe his or her energy, courage, and light into your body for at least ten minutes. Now get up. Do something you have been afraid to face or deal with. Notice how you feel in extensive detail.

Protection

As a graduate of the school of hard knocks, I have found I regularly need to create a safe, protected environment. Such a space supports me in moving through whatever fears may emerge. Human beings have a primal need to feel safe. It is important to honor this need, finding alternatives to weapons, locks, and elaborate security systems.

How can I create a deeper sense of protection?

Perhaps the greatest source of protection is your integrity. Having integrity is living in wholeness with yourself and your environment. It does not require you to lead an absolutely perfect life. Perfection is not for human beings. It is what we strive for.

When you know you are living to contribute to the well-being of others and your environment, there is an increased sense of integrity. Cultivating good intentions toward others, being true to your principles, honoring your inner divinity and imperfections, refraining from unnecessary criticism of others, and performing actions in the spirit of service contribute to your sense of protection. Do not misunderstand this. Nothing guarantees that unpleasant or even dangerous circumstances will never occur. Nevertheless, your good actions in the present can help nullify the power of negative past or future Karma, allowing you to experience protection in even the direst circumstances. Let me explain this a little further.

Past impressions of your good actions, called *samskaras* in Sanskrit, become part of your aura, or energy field. One day, they will bear positive fruit in your life. The following story from ancient India illustrates this.

In ancient times, a shipwrecked man, completely disheveled and starving, found himself in a strange land. The palace guards discovered him and immediately brought him to their king. They assumed the king would imprison and punish this odd-looking, filthy, smelly stranger who was of a different race because strangers were unwelcome in this land. However, the king was a very wise man. He intuitively knew he was in the presence of a kind, loving being. He saw light radiating from the man's eyes and forehead. With great respect, the king had the man bathed, perfumed, clothed in finery, fed well, and housed in luxurious quarters in the royal palace. The king's great generosity astounded the guards. It turns out the stranger had led a life of compassionate service to his family, friends, and community and had regularly performed spiritual practices. As a result, his Karma attracted benevolent circumstances that saved his life.

If you think that example is a bit remote from real life, consider this one. For ten years, I studied healing techniques and meditation at a school called actualism, which uses inner light/fire for healing and transmutation. In my training, I was eventually given spiritual tools for protection. Years later, boarding a flight in London for Los Angeles, I heard about riots taking place in the city of my destination. During the very long flight, I vomited twice, an unusual occurrence for me. I asked myself, "Why am I upset? Could it be the riots?" Throughout my life, I had often experienced intense physical reactions before significant events.

Riding in a taxi from LAX, it became obvious as we neared the epicenter of the riots. Smoke blanketed the entire area. It was quite surreal. As we inched forward, I noticed gangs of young people roaming the streets. A few pressed against the taxi window growling, "We're going to kill you." The driver was deeply frightened. I sensed he was a Holocaust survivor. Silently and telepathically, I was able to calm him down. My inner guidance told me to repeat my Siddha Yoga mantra, to be perfectly still and inwardly place my actualism spiritual protection around me. Following these directions, I felt a sensation of total stillness and peaceful detachment.

Because I did not play the role of victim, the would-be killers could not assume their role. They were waiting for a fearful response to fuel their fury. Because the driver and I did not respond, they quickly disappeared into the smoky evening. My spiritual tools of protection have literally saved my life many times.

Guidelines for Dealing with Fear

1. Acknowledge to yourself that you are experiencing fear. Locate the fear in your body.

2. Breathing consciously, allow the fear to move through your body. Send the fear to your legs, feet, toes, and fingers. Disperse it through your body. You may want to shake out your hands or stamp your feet.

3. Do not think of yourself as being afraid. Rather, think of yourself as having fear. (I have fear…I have worry…I have anxiety…and so forth.) This subtle distinction has great power because it maintains your identity as separate from your transitory emotional experience.

4. Take long, slow, deep breaths as you observe your environment. Be in the now.

5. Connect to your spiritual power. Invoke protection in your own way (for example, repeat your mantra or a meaningful prayer, engage in visualization, and so forth).

6. Take the next appropriate action as you move through your fear, or remain completely still. Do nothing until it is appropriate.

Transforming Fear into Creativity: Written Contemplation

1. Where is fear holding you back in life? How are you procrastinating?

2. If you confront your fear, what are you afraid will occur?

3. What does this fear remind you of from the past?

4. What appropriate action can you take now?

5. Are you willing to take that action?

6. In your imagination take that action. Feel it as if it is happening in your body. Experience the fear transmuting into creative energy.

7.   Are there any other positive choices you can make? Create your own strategy. Listen for guidance. Write down these responses.

Creativity is the freedom to respond with different, unique choices to the circumstances life presents, and you always have that freedom.

4

Living with Your Personal Power

What does it mean for you to live and express your personal power?

There are probably hundreds of books on this subject. First, let us discover what personal power is not. Personal power is not controlling or coercing others to do what you want them to. It is not the freedom to dump all of your anger and pent-up frustration on others. It is not about always winning and/or never taking no for an answer. These tactics are common misinterpretations of personal power. I have seen graduates of some weekend self-help trainings, for example, forcefully sharing their experiences and pressuring friends to sign up for the same course. Group leaders may have encouraged them to share their experience of the course or said they were not owning their personal power.

Don't you spontaneously want to share something great that you've discovered? Won't others naturally gravitate to those who are fully alive and enlightened?

There is a difference between sharing and proselytizing. The willingness or unwillingness of others to receive information must always be respected. Individuals who ignore this can become New Age bulldozers, demanding the world give them what they want at all times. They are committed to always speak up and always go for what the desire. This is not personal power. It is narcissism.

Isn't it important to have the courage to ask for what you want in life?

For those who have historically been passive and silent, giving yourself permission to ask for what you want and need is certainly a positive development. That is different from forcing your opinions on others or demanding what you want in a loud, abrasive way. Personal power is not about being selfish and demanding wherever you go.

What is your definition of personal power then?

Personal power can be summed up as compassionate self-expression. Compassionate self-expression is creative rather than destructive, supportive rather than judgmental. When you authentically express yourself, others are positively affected, moved, and inspired. You have made a positive contribution. The more you are able to employ compassionate self-expression, the more you will experience your personal power. Void of concern for others, your expression would be selfish and egotistical. We do not live in isolation. It is quite the opposite. We are connected to everyone and everything. Life is about being in a relationship, moment to moment, to something. It may be a person, animal, plant, object, country, or universe itself. Through compassionate self-expression, you are always sensitive to your environment, respectful of humanity and nature.

All of us have the spark of divinity within. Each of us needs to find a personal way to express truth. Though spiritual energy resides in all of our hearts, the form of its outer expression is always unique. Isn't that amazing? We have all been given this freedom to individually express our personal power. Personal power is an ongoing process you must continuously renew with the power of your intention. Ask yourself where you want to go in life and what you want to express today. Then act in alignment with your wishes by committing yourself to finding appropriate vehicles for self-expression.

It all sounds so daunting. What if I don't have a great talent to make a significant contribution? How can I experience my personal power?

Some people do experience personal power in their creative work; others may view them as brimming with personal power. However, the same talented people may not experience personal power in their day-to-day lives, especially in relationships with others, because there is no form to personal power. You do not have to be brilliant. Personal power resides in your inner experience of compassionate self-expression. Everyone can express his or her personal power at every moment, despite your life circumstances.

The Third *Chakra*

Seven nonphysical energy centers are around your body, conducting life force energy. In Sanskrit, these are called *chakras*, or wheels of light. They are located:

- At the base of your spine (physical survival)

- Below your navel (emotional/sexual survival)

- At your solar plexus (personal power)

- Your heart (unconditional love)

- Throat (clear communication)

- Between your eyebrows, also known as the third eye (clear perception)

- At the crown of your head (connection to the cosmos)

The color of the third *chakra* is yellow, also the color traditionally associated with courage. This combination is not an accident. It takes great courage to express your personal power.

When *shakti*, or life force energy, streams through this *chakra*, you experience the power within to live your truth. Each *chakra* has an associated sound. The sound equated with the third *chakra* is *hrum* (hrōōm). When chanted with intention, this sound raises the vibration of its *chakra*. People often report experiencing a buzzing in their solar plexus when expressing their personal power. After intensively studying the teaching of the great masters and giving sessions to literally thousands of people, as well as from my own experience, I have found that personal power has nine essential components.

Nine Components of Personal Power

1. Communication/Sharing Your Truth

The Bible proclaims the truth shall set you free. When you articulate from your own experience, people will know where you stand. You are free to be aligned with your truth. It is your responsibility to share your truth if you want to experience your personal power; however, many of us do not know what our truth really is. It is so easy to fall into the trap of overtalking and overgeneralizing our feelings and opinions. It is important to understand that sharing your truth does not justify telling everyone what you are feeling or thinking at all times. Statements like, "Joe is a jerk," "Dan is pervert," or "New York City is a jungle" are spurious and do not serve you well.

To know our truth, we must be silent. Sadly, the cell phone is seriously compromising privacy and respect for silence in our society. Television advertisements encourage us to call people on our cell phones every chance we get, including while in public. Boundaries between what is public and what is private are breaking down at an alarming rate. We are becoming a society of overtalkers and loud-talkers. Parks were created as sanctuaries for peace and quiet, but a stroll in the park nowadays includes listening to other people's phone conversations because so many cell phone users apparently feel they must amp up their volume to be heard. Every coffee shop is now filled with people loudly talking on cell phones. For years, I relished having time to read and write in the peace and quiet of these establishments. Now it is often a challenge to stay focused.

How closely do you listen to what you are saying or hearing? Have you ever observed what happens to your energy when you continue talking after rejecting an outer or inner message to be silent? Too much talking drains your life force. Especially when gossiping and slandering the reputation of others, notice what happens to your state of mind. Are you really practicing freedom of speech, or are you merely speaking at will? Listening without adequate rest is also draining. Notice how you feel after a long, intensive period of listening to others talk.

Our society tends to encourage impulsive behavior instead of thoughtful contemplation. Even though it is tempting to blurt out whatever you're thinking, you may sometimes live to regret it. If you think carefully before speaking, it is actually easier to share your truth, particularly about emotional issues. Your words are literally sound vibrations with the power to disturb or uplift those around you. Instead of blurting out judgmental remarks ("You make me angry" or "You make me crazy"), with contemplation, there is time to dig deeper into what is really true. You then might share, "When you said that, I felt angry because I have a need for you to respect me and I feel criticized." You might say, "When you don't call me back, I have a fear I'll never see you again." No one except yourself is the source of your experience. Of course, all of us need to be continually reminded of this.

Dharma means living in accordance with the divine will, or, literally, "what holds together." *Dharmic* communication entails taking responsibility for your entire experience, including your thoughts, ideas, emotions, and opinions. To support clearer, nonattacking communication, I recommend studying Marshall

Rosenberg's guidebook, *Non-Violent Communication*, for a deeper understanding of this subject.

2.   Sharing Your Creative Gifts

Many of us have been shamed and humiliated for expressing our creativity. "Stay in the lines!" was the commandment we followed while coloring with crayons at Joseph Warren Elementary in Chicago. "That does not look like a person!" shouted an art teacher looking at a child's drawing of her father. "You are tone-deaf. You can't sing!" a choir director pronounced to a humiliated young girl in front of her peers. Verbal judgments of children by those in positions of authority cause deep, negative impressions. The child may decide, "It is too painful to share my creative gifts in front of others. I will never do this again."

Perhaps the most direct way to experience your personal power is sharing your creative gifts with others. You may never sound like Andrea Boccelli or Celine Dion, but you can still sing for your own pleasure. Self-expression is good, even essential, for your spirit. If you withhold your creative gifts, you are closeting a part of your soul. Part of our function as human beings is to create, but the creation does not have to be award-winning or of museum quality to fulfill this need.

Some of my retreats and workshops provided a safe environment for students to express themselves through storytelling, dancing, acting, singing, drawing, and painting. At first, some were afraid to perform in front of the group. Once they confronted their fears, a noticeable shift occurred. When they discovered they were not shamed or humiliated, participants felt accepted. Most experienced pleasure in their self-expression. For some, it even became more painful not to participate, and they radiated enthusiasm through the experience of getting up in front of a group.

After the workshop, beautiful, creative experiences occurred in the participants' lives. Students began singing, playing instruments, writing music, painting, and speaking in public. Some had the courage to begin performing in clubs. Courageous, pleasurable self-expression became part of their lives. As we move through our fears and share our creative gifts, life becomes an exciting adventure.

3.   Living Your Truth

Living your truth includes what you say and eat, where you live and work, your choice of friends, intimate relationships, habits, and so forth. Everything you do can be an expression of your personal power.

Other examples of living your truth are not as obvious, requiring greater contemplation. For example, if you have friends whose constant negativity is draining you, it is time to reconsider what value you receive from the relationships. When you know in your heart that you cannot support working for a company with unethical business practices, it is appropriate to find another job. If you detest urban living, it may be appropriate for you to relocate to more natural surroundings or to create urban gardens in your community.

Although challenging in the short run, ultimately addressing these things can mean having friends who support you and enhance your life, being proud of the work you do, or living where you most desire, amidst colors, furnishings, and styles that most reflect your taste and preferences.

4.   Living with Integrity in Your World

Every thought, word, or action you have affects those around you. You can honor your commitments to yourself and others without becoming extremist or self-righteous. If you agree to meet someone at a particular time, it is important to honor your agreement. Consistently keeping one's agreements with others establishes trust.

Politically, there may be causes you do not wish to support. Knowing that certain companies discriminate against minorities may prevent you from purchasing their goods. The choice is yours to make.

The earth is a living entity with a soul. It is time for us to expand our consciousness beyond our immediate neighborhood to include caring for the planet and all of its inhabitants. When a bomb drops thousands of miles away, we are all affected. When nuclear testing occurs, the vibrations affect the earth and all of its inhabitants. We are all in relationship on this earth, a connected, integral part of the whole.

Living with integrity, with the awareness of interconnectedness, you vibrate certainty. You do your best to not harm others. There is a saying in twelve-step programs, "Walk your walk, and talk your talk." In other words, have integrity in your life. You are not going to do this perfectly, but you can immediately clean up any messes you create, becoming part of the solution to the world's problems.

5.   Have Faith in Yourself to Do the Right Thing

In our extremely competitive society, it can look as if the only way to attain success is to step over others, wheel and deal, and "get them before they get you." This attitude breeds contempt and is based on distrust of yourself, others, and universe. If you do not respect your own motivations and are operating from greed and manipulation, it is likely you will project this lack of respect on others, assuming this is the world's modus operandi of everyone is also out to get you. Needless to say, paranoia is not a solid foundation from which to operate.

The need to control others comes from feelings of powerlessness, the antithesis of personal power, and is a misuse of your resources. Intelligence and creativity are not weapons to be used over others. Based on the law of Karma, when you manipulate others, you are planting seeds to attract the same experience on the other side of the equation, thus setting yourself up to be used.

Breaking this cycle requires faith. You need faith in yourself to know what your appropriate actions are. You also need faith in God or the universe that you will be guided toward the higher road in life.

6.   Risking Disapproval and Conflict

Have you ever noticed how, after satisfactorily making a major decision, you feel a surge of good energy, opportunities begin appearing, and someone eventually challenges your choice? It is a cosmic law that, if you take a strong position, whether for or against something, you will eventually attract someone who vehemently disagrees with you. According to metaphysical law, opposites really do attract. This is another example of a behavior pattern that can leave you stuck in a seemingly endless loop of conflict. It is as if you are a piece on a chessboard. Once you change your position, in order to win, your opponent must change his position. Until someone relinquishes winning as a goal, the situation will recycle.

In this world, the dominant ego game is, "I want to be right." The flaw in this thinking is that, in order for someone to be right, others must be wrong. According to this logic, if Christians are right, then Jews, Muslims, Buddhists, and atheists must be wrong. If heterosexuality is right, then homosexuality and bisexuality must be wrong and so on.

Instead of viewing life as a battle, you can choose to converse with those who disagree with you. Through dialogue and by treating others with respect, you can discover common ground with others, while still acknowledging your differences. Being true to yourself invites the risk of disapproval. Despite receiving the disapproval of others as you live your truth, you can choose not to control others and not allow others to manipulate you. You can grant others their beliefs and opinions as you express your truth.

During the New York City 2004 Republican Convention, I heard several people say, "I don't want them in my city. They have no right to be here." It saddened me because this only feeds division in the world. If we can't peacefully live beside those we disagree with here at home, how will there ever be world peace?

As you advance on your spiritual path, you will be tested. Instead of abandoning the path of conscious living, you can strengthen your resolve to live your truth and fulfill your purpose, no matter what.

7. Acknowledging Your Spiritual Connection

On some days, our ego wants us to believe that we literally create everything through the power of our intention. In New Age jargon, it is common to hear, "I created that parking space," or "I created a great lover." Did you create, or did you attract it?

When your life is flowing and your goals and desires are manifesting around you, it is so easy to become heady and ecstatic. Yes, it is wonderful when things you have been working and praying for begin materializing. When this transpires in my life, I acknowledge myself for my efforts. I am always compelled to thank Mother/Father God, the universe, the Siddhas, and angelic beings for the grace in my life.

As you become more synchronized with the universe and your individual purpose, amazing things will occur. The world becomes a friendly place. You are met with smiles everywhere. People extend generosity to you in so many ways. You are the recipient of great benefits.

I believe the great successes and happiness in my life are due to my personal efforts and my spiritual practices, especially chanting and meditation. I have received phenomenal value from chanting the Siddha Yoga mantras and the Buddhist mantra, Nam Myoho Renge Kyo, which means, "I am devoted to the mystic law of cause and effect in the universe through sound."

Some people give one hundred percent credit for their good fortune to God or higher power, but we can also acknowledge how our actively chosen, positive efforts attract blessings. It is all right to acknowledge yourself and your spiritual connection concurrently.

8. The Power of Silence

It is said that silence is the language of God and the language of love. It is said that it speaks louder than words. Your presence and listening often make a greater difference than your words. Unfortunately, many of us have difficulty remaining silent. Notice the masses of people constantly plugged into their iPods or CD players as they simultaneously perform other tasks. The ceaseless chatter is an obstacle that isolates us and diminishes our energy, whereas silence cultivates and increases our life force energy. This is why there is great focus on maintaining silence in monasteries and ashrams worldwide. After extensive chanting, monks, nuns, and participants become very quiet and still. They are naturally led to meditation. It is said that chanting leads to prayer. Prayer produces the state of meditation. Meditation leads to the depths of silence.

Silence supports *Ātma Vichāra*, the Sanskrit word for self-inquiry. As you contemplate your life in silence, amazing insights will occur. Silence also protects you from speaking inappropriately or indiscriminately. Silence even has the power to protect you from performing harmful actions. Silence is truly refreshing to the mind, body, and spirit. In my busy schedule, I practice silence one day a week as often as possible.

9.   Magnetic and Dynamic

Two essential qualities provide equilibrium in our lives. In the school of actualism, they are called the magnetic and the dynamic. The magnetic quality is referred to as the feminine, receptive, or yin energy. The magnetic innately attracts that which it desires. This may include love, attention, approval, affection, and recognition. The magnetic does not push outwardly to manifest results. Stillness, being, listening, and receiving are the attributes of the magnetic.

On the other hand, the dynamic quality is associated with the male, active, or yang energy. The dynamic moves forward, thrusting itself into interactions with others, moving toward a goal. Action is required. The dynamic is about doing. Contemporary society resonates so loudly with the dynamic, condoning aggressive tactics in the business world that we may be in danger of becoming human doings. Without an equal amount of the magnetic, we are lopsided.

Nevertheless, distrust of the magnetic permeates our society. How can you trust people to be there for you when they are imperfect? If you open up, you may be shamed, humiliated, abused, or just plain disappointed. How can you draw what you need to yourself from the universe when you have been let down so often? Therefore, some conclude they must become completely self-reliant. "The heck with receiving! I'll just take care of myself," they say.

Personal power is the balanced integration of these two qualities. You dynamically express yourself, compassionately moving through your fears as you relate to the world around you. You do what needs to be done. At the same time, you can magnetically receive love, support, nurturing, and inspiration from your environment. Life is about doing and being as well as giving and receiving.

You are both magnetic and dynamic. The cosmic union of yin and yang takes place within yourself. As you bring these qualities together in harmony, you will have a more direct experience of your true personal power.

Living with Your Personal Power: Written Contemplation

1. Where in your life are you fully sharing your experience and truth? When do you withhold from sharing your experiences and opinions? Do you offer your opinions when people around you are not interested in them?

2. Are you flowing your creative gifts and talents out? Do you only express your creativity behind closed doors? Do you ever share your talents or creations with others?

3. Are you living where you want to live? Are you doing the work/making the contribution you desire?

4. Do your friendships and romantic relationships fulfill you?

5. Do you have a harmonious relationship with your environment? Are you a part of the solution to the world's problems? How are you contributing to the world's problems?

6. How do you control or manipulate others? It may be very subtle or very obvious. If you let that control go, what are you afraid would happen?

7. Do you risk taking actions because of the fear of disapproval? Do you withhold your truth and creativity because of fear? If so, how?

8. Do you acknowledge your imperfections? What about your strengths?

9. Can you remain silent for a long period of time? Do you allow yourself long stretches of quiet?

Magnetic/Dynamic Exercise

1. Imagine your right side is expanding beyond your body. On the right side of your energy field is the presence of your dynamic energy. Tune into this. Do

you see or sense a presence? It may be subtle. Ask your dynamic energy how it would like you to put yourself out in the world. Ask for its support.

2.   Imagine the presence of your magnetic energy is on your left side. Tune into this. Do you sense a form, shape, or body? Do you feel a presence? Whatever you feel, see, or sense is perfect. Ask your magnetic energy how it would like to be expressed. What does it want to receive in your life? Ask for your magnetic energy's support and guidance.

3.   Use your imagination to create the experience of your magnetic and dynamic energies in greater harmony.

Compassionate self-expression determines the degree you will experience your personal power. Void of any concern for others, your expression could be considered selfish and egotistical.

5

Opening Your Heart to Receive Love

Many of my clients have asked for advice on how to have a more loving relationship or find a soul mate. They share how they constantly attract unavailable or undesirable partners. Some are so frustrated by having no dating or love life at all that they cry out, "Why is this happening to me?"

No matter what you profess, you are either willing to open up and have a positive relationship or hold on to past relationships. If the latter is true, it does not matter whether past experiences were positive or negative. If you insist on maintaining old attachments of any kind, you are not aligned to have a new, loving relationship. It is doubtful that one will occur until you open your heart.

Isn't it true that some people, especially very spiritual people, are meant to be celibate? Isn't it true that some people will never have romantic relationships and should just give up?

Perhaps some people are meant to be celibate. Some monks, nuns, and priests are very comfortable with their vow of celibacy. Some people I know in their late fifties or sixties are perfectly content never having sex or romantic relationships again. This, however, seems to be more of an exception.

When you have a long, dry spell, it is tempting to ask, "Is this my destiny? Am I supposed to be alone and celibate by default for the rest of my life? Is this the divine plan for me?" As you surrender to the intricacies of a more spiritual life path, it may be appropriate to experience a cycle of celibacy. In this context, celibacy means choosing to not be sexually active, date, or pursue romantic relationships. After a series of confusing or dissatisfying relationships, some choose to stop turning the wheel of endless frustration and practice celibacy for a while.

Celibacy is a way of ceasing to have your vital energies deeply enmeshed with another person's. This separation allows you to recover your own life force energy. Choosing not to be sexually active gives you the opportunity to find new ways of relating to others. This enables you to:

- Have more time for spiritual practices and study.

- Delve into creative projects.

- Discover your truth and clarify your priorities.

- Replenish your body and rest.

- Heal emotional wounds.

- Increase your reservoir of spiritual energy.

It is sometimes valuable to practice celibacy with your partner for a period of time, enhancing the nonsexual aspects of the relationship. In this case, celibacy means refraining from sexual acts, but it does not prohibit affection. Sex can be used as a profound vehicle for communication or avoiding deep communication and going unconscious. Consciously abstaining for a time can provide perspective on the role that sex plays in your relationship.

Does timing play a major role in having a relationship?

As the saying goes, "There is a time for all things." Life is about cycles. You will have your time for love and intimacy. Just as your cycle of intimacy needs to be honored, so does your time for solitude.

If an intimate relationship is not happening right now, you do not need to go into resistance. Don't fight your life circumstances because this will waste your vital energy. Accept what is, and concentrate on other interests. Learn to relish your solitude.

Life can be so funny. When the beloved appears, it may be when it is very unexpected. So many people meet their mate while simply focusing on living. Shopping for love is the farthest thing from their mind, even later in life. James Brolin said he was quite content, accepting being alone, before he met his future wife, Barbra Streisand. This is quite common.

Others have reported their beloved appeared at an inopportune time, such as while they were in another relationship, traveling, ill, dealing with illness or death in the family, facing unemployment, or a myriad of other scenarios. Perhaps you need to have certain life experiences before your beloved will appear. One client needed to pursue a goal of studying acting for fun and found her beloved in that class.

Is it possible for everyone who wants a long-term relationship to have one?

I won't say it's impossible. At the same time, I do not believe it is the Karma of everyone to have a long-term romantic relationship. A small percentage of you will be celibate. Some will move through a series of relationships. Some will experience phenomenal closeness with a friend or teacher that is not romantic, but deeply fulfilling nevertheless. This is love as well. This is a significant relationship, even if it is not sexual. Still others will be grounded in a long-term partnership. Each of you will have your own lessons, obstacles, and joys on your path.

Knowing your personal astrology and numerology can help reveal the Karma you were born with regarding relationships. I think of numerology and astrology as coded information, blueprints we arrived with on this earth. However, these are tools, not rigid rules. Remember, through your thoughts, words, and actions, you have the power to change your Karma right now.

What are the obstacles to having a wonderful, loving relationship?

The most significant obstacles to experiencing deep love and intimacy are the fears lodged in your subconscious. Let us examine these fears.

Intimacy and Solitude

For many, the prospect of intimacy is frightening. Think about it. Intimacy: Into-Me-See. A part of you may feel hesitant to share very private pieces of the puzzle of your identity. Some of you only feel comfortable or safe when locked in a permanent smile, only exhibiting your sweeter, kinder side to others. Does this sound like you? You do not want to share your fears and upsets. You do not want to shake things up. You want to stay positive, regardless of what happens. If you do this, you may pray your uncomfortable feelings will disappear. Believe me, this will not happen.

We all have a shadow or dark side. Because being truly intimate with another requires vulnerability and being vulnerable dissolves your masks of pretension, exposing all of you, it may feel risky. There is no way around this, but being fully present and seen in a relationship can elicit great healing if you allow it. In one of her recent films, Susan Sarandon remarked the purpose of relationship is to have someone witness your life. How true! Having a witness is validating and quite profound. As humans, we seek this witness. Nevertheless, hidden parts of your identity may be afraid to step into the light because, the more you expose yourself, the greater the risk of rejection. Because this is true, if you want deeper relationships of any kind, face it, and get over it.

Some of us shield ourselves from raw, naked self-expression except in times of crisis, when the walls come tumbling down, or occasionally during lovemaking. Holding back reduces the possibility of intimacy, which automatically implies sharing and receptivity. We are vessels for receiving the opinions, moods, jealousies, stories, fears, peculiarities, excesses, and pleasantries of others.

It may sometimes be uncomfortable to spend time with someone in very close proximity. It may feel stifling or claustrophobic. You may not want to have someone, even your beloved, in your space. You may not want to have to relate to another person for such a long period. Some people even flee after periods of intimate time together, longing to be alone.

While it is also a very human desire to crave solitude, it does not have to be an "all or nothing" proposition. I relish time alone and peaceful silence. Daily, I try providing a quiet oasis for myself. When outer circumstances prevent me from having privacy and solitude, I will claim it on long walks by myself.

Some of us have a greater desire for solitude than intimacy. Yet, it is desirable and pleasurable to acquire both intimacy and solitude in a balance that is comfortable for you. My parents, married for more than sixty-nine years before my dad died, were a living example of a couple who held both intimacy and solitude in their relationship. Perhaps this was the secret of their longevity. In my dad's office, he wrote books and plays, read, and watched CNN and sporting events for hours. My mom enjoyed her lanai for growing plants, reading, and contemplating. My parents spent time both together and apart throughout the day. My dad exercised regularly and played golf three times a week. My mom taught exercise at a nursing home. They had an active social life as well.

Not every couple can afford to have separate rooms, so honoring solitude may require creative solutions, like solitary walks in nature and visiting places or friends separately. Each partner should be encouraged to pursue his or her own interests. Blocks of shared intimate time are often not readily available in our frenetic lifestyles, it is essential to take care of distractions so you can find an appropriate balance between intimacy and solitude.

Togetherness Exercise

Slow down with your partner, and simply be together. Turn off cell phones, beepers, television, radio, CD players, and computers. Close your eyes. Facing each other, place your hands on each other's heart. Take nine full, long breaths together. Open your eyes. Take another nine full, long breaths together. Remain silent. Your silence is your solitude. Your joining together is your intimacy. With practice, you can cultivate both.

Loss of Identity

Isn't the nature of opening about merging together? Doesn't love dissolve the sense of separation? Must we lose ourselves when we love fully? How can you be yourself and totally love another?

These are good questions to ponder. The fear of losing oneself in a relationship has mystified humankind for eons. When you have cultivated a sense of self, it is safer to focus on another without losing your identity. You need to know yourself, including your tastes, likes, dislikes, opinions, and truth. This requires a great deal of contemplation.

During moments of merging with another, there is great ecstasy. Ego is absent. There is pure consciousness. This is why relationships are a pathway to the divine. After merging, you will eventually return to your normal state of consciousness, aware of your physical boundaries. You will once again experience your separate identity.

When you do not know who you are, it is quite tempting to escape into a relationship. Some become the person their partner wants them to be. There is a structure, script, or role to play. They feel saved from doing the work necessary to find out who they really are. They do not have to take responsibility for their own truth. They remain in their comfort zone without stretching or testing their opinions, ideas, and beliefs. It takes at least a lifetime to discover who you really are, deepening your sense of self as you share your life with others.

Emotional Trauma

Equally inhibiting to love and intimacy can be the emotional trauma you carry in your cells, organs, muscles, and connective tissue. You can do something positive about this. To deal with your emotional trauma, become aware of it. Then be willing to let it go. Otherwise, it will keep showing up in your life, sabotaging opportunities for health, love, and intimacy. You will act out your unresolved emotions repeatedly. This is the universe's way of saying, "Deal with it." You have a choice. Open up to be supported in dealing with your trauma. Bodywork, Reiki, soul retrieval, somatic therapy, and energy work can release accumulated emotional trauma. Working with other healers has been invaluable for me and well worth the financial investment.

Physical and Sexual Abuse

Impressions of physical and sexual abuse penetrate deeply into the core of your being. Even when the memories are suppressed, the energy of the incidents remains. If this is part of your experience, you need to find ways of facing it and resolving your emotional wounds. Sexual and physical abuse can be so damaging that you may subconsciously radiate your trauma to others. Without knowing why, you may attract potential perpetrators to re-create a new version of the original trauma.

I present this information not to induce feelings of guilt, but to assist you in finding a way out of your suffering and misery. If you have experienced physical or sexual abuse, as many of us have to some degree, at least be willing to see how it may be negatively affecting your health and relationships. You do not need to remain victimized by the past.

Despite a history of physical and/or sexual abuse, it is still possible to have a loving, intimate relationship. Several of my clients have proven this. They have changed their relationship Karma. While nothing can erase the scars from the past, dealing with the trauma and transforming it can pave the way for successful, fulfilling relationships.

Fear of Humiliation and Rejection

When you experience humiliation as a child, you probably do not feel safe to express your anger and pain in that moment. The child closes down his or her true feelings, creating a pattern of withholding. Years later, this pattern still may be unwittingly locked in place. Unfortunately, withholding does not attract love or intimacy. If you are baffled as to why you are not in an intimate relationship, withholding may be the culprit.

Some of us spend lives of quiet seclusion to avoid uncomfortable and confrontational situations. Still others will engage in brief, intense sexual connect and then leave to avoid any possibility of true intimacy. Do you embody either of these patterns?

Exposing yourself to the intricacies of a relationship opens you to possible rejection. Every time you experience rejection because of your race, physical appearance, religion, political beliefs, sexual orientation, handicap, or weaknesses, an impression is embedded in your aura. The next time you risk rejection, your memories will be reactivated. You may choose either to close down or feel the fear of humiliation or rejection. The second choice allows you to remain open to the intimacy you crave.

Despite past rejection, humiliation, abuse, loss of identity, the need for solitude, or bad timing, you can uproot the weeds that have gathered around your heart. You have the choice to remain open to love today.

Opening Your Heart to Receive Love: Written Contemplation

1. Are you open to receive love and intimacy? Do you flee from available potential mates? Do you close down, negate yourself, or go numb when someone expresses love for you?

2. Are you currently receiving love and intimacy? If not, why do you think this is so? What choices have you made that are contributing to this?

3. What are you afraid will transpire, or what do you fear losing, if you allow love and intimacy into your life?

4. Are you willing to release past hurts and open yourself to receive love now? Do you feel this isn't the right time? Why? What do you have to do or become to receive love and intimacy?

The Beaming Exercise

I have shared this exercise with hundreds of clients. It is designed to make you more magnetic and receptive to love and intimacy. Please keep in mind that you sometimes have unresolved Karma to work through with others before your beloved appears. Keep your heart open, keep breathing, keep loving yourself, and know that whoever appears on your path is perfect for your growth. There is always a lesson to be learned. This does not mean you need to become romantically involved with whoever comes along. Instead, ask yourself, "What can I contribute to this person?" If you are thoroughly honest with yourself, the answers will be revealed to you. Trust you will know when you are with your beloved.

Clients practicing the beaming exercise have shared the following results:

• Those who previously had no dating life began dating.

• Those already in a relationship either made a more solid commitment to it or moved on to meet their beloved.

• Everyone felt more attractive and magnetic.

At the very least, this exercise can assist you in accelerating the process of meeting your beloved. Remember, your beloved is not perfect. He or she is not the answer to your problems. However, you have a resonance together that will stimulate your greatest growth. When you find your beloved, a new process will begin to unfold.

Nightly Practice

1. Imagine you are standing atop the tallest point in your vicinity. In nature, this is a great cliff, hill, or mountaintop. In cities, this would be the Eiffel Tower, the Empire State Building, Griffith Park Observatory, and so forth.

2. Imagine a ruby-red searchlight is emanating from your chest.

3. Declare, "I am now willing to receive you, my beloved, into my life."

4. Beam out the searchlight three times clockwise.

5. Imagine it is evening and millions of lights are twinkling. One of those twinkling lights represents your beloved.

6. Declare, "I am thrilled to receive you now, my beloved. You are available, and we both desire being together. Come to me now!"

7. Open your heart and the left side of your body to receive. Your beloved is beaming back to you. Intensify this connection in your heart. You might feel heat, tingling, or excitement. Focus on receiving for five minutes. Stay in a meditative, receptive state. Notice what impressions or messages come to you.

Morning Practice

1. Before leaving home, declare, "I ask God (or the universe) to guide me today to be in the most auspicious circumstances to receive my beloved in my life."

2. Trust your intuition. If you hear your inner voice directing you to go somewhere that day (to a party, the supermarket, for a walk, to the espresso bar), go! You never know who you will meet. Have fun with it.

6

How Gratitude Draws Grace into Your Life

What is grace?

I define grace as the presence of love, protection, and healing in the universe. Grace is one of my very favorite words. To many, Jesus and Mary are embodiments of grace. For others, Shakyamuni Buddha is. Still others, a guru like Gurumayi or the Dalai Lama is. I have felt the presence of grace in times of celebration (which was easy) and hardship (not so easy).

Years ago, I felt helpless, powerless, unloved, unsuccessful, and financially stressed. It seemed as if everything was falling apart around me. I kept resisting the outer circumstances, and things grew worse. The more I tried controlling my outer environment, the more dismal things became. The voice of my inner guru said, "Surrender. Accept what is happening. Be grateful for what you have."

I was then guided to journey into my deepest fears. I cried, and it was most uncomfortable going to that place. To my surprise, a pervasive serenity began engulfing me. In that instant, I could accept my life circumstances. Life was okay as it was. I was okay as I was. Peace of mind followed surrender and acceptance.

Astonishingly, in the outer world, things abruptly improved. Money long overdue arrived in the mail. The phone practically rang off the hook with people booking sessions. From around the country, several people called, thanking me for the positive difference Damienwork made in their lives. This was grace, the beacon of light amidst the darkness. This proved to me how every challenging situation is a powerful vehicle for transformation.

Gratitude, like selfless service, has the attributes of being a spiritual practice. Society designates good or bad qualities to the multitude of life circumstances. The outer circumstances then determine your emotional responses. However, gratitude invites you to receive benefit from whatever life is offering. This perspective puts you in charge of your emotional responses.

Practicing gratitude increases your awareness. Stepping back from the often harsh realities of life, you can reflect on what the hidden blessings may be. Even when things appear to be hopeless, grace is present. While choosing to recognize greater, unseen forces at work, gratitude embraces the totality of the human condition. Inner feelings of gratitude lead to outer expressions of respect. When you are truly grateful for the miraculous workings of your body, it is natural to treat it with respect. You will desire more nourishing foods, invigorating exercise, and substantial rest. Due to gratitude, the grace of your body will sustain you in times of great stress.

The Native American tradition is particularly rich with ceremonies that honor the earth. Immense gratitude is expressed for nature's bountiful blessings. These ceremonies evoke a reverence for animals and all living things, as well as of the elements. Native American tradition teaches Mother Earth will demonstrate her grace with rain and sunshine, creating an abundant harvest if you regularly honor and respect her. The relationship between humans and the earth here is one of mutual appreciation.

The gardens we cultivate literally and symbolically, both inside and outside our homes, are sacred. They support our well-being and protect us from the severity of the elements providing shelter, warmth, or coolness. Our homes also supply an environment for necessary solitude, rest prayer, meditation, and contemplation. Sleeping in our beds, we process many of our unresolved issues. Our homes are the physical foundation for our inner and outer lives.

Do you treat your home with respect? Are you grateful for what your home provides, even if you live in a tiny room? Do you keep your home in order? Does your home feel harmonious or beautiful? As exemplified in the Chinese art of feng shui, our homes have their own unique spirits. Within the walls are the vibrations of all that has transpired there. When you have gratitude, harmony, and respect for your home, you will experience its grace, its soul. Your home will reward you with peace and comfort.

You may also reflect with gratitude on the wonderful people in your life, including your family, acquaintances, friends, and others. Honoring your loved ones is a humbling practice. You may choose to express your love and appreciation to these people directly. Thanking others for their presence in your life enables you to view your relationships from a higher perspective. Through receiving your acknowledgement, the person feels your gratitude. Both of you experience the value of your relationship. Seeing life with the eyes of gratitude illuminates your reality. Do you feel underappreciated in your job? Look for what is positive there, even if you must look hard. Someone or something must be positive. It is like hunting for a hidden treasure. If you stay with it, you will find gold.

Opportunities for Growth/Enlightenment

When I adopt the attitude that everything is grace and every moment of life is perfect as it is, I experience serenity. It may seem odd, but surrendering to the pits of despair actually precipitated greater faith and fearlessness for me. The obstacles around you, whether they are humorous or aggravating, are the perfect vehicles for your growth. Pain can be a signal to go within and find the source of your unhappiness so you can do something about it.

Cultivating gratitude for physical and emotional challenges unveils the subtle gifts hidden there. My dear friend, Orah, now legally blind, has profoundly deepened her spiritual sight, becoming a talented healer, interfaith minister, and singer/composer. She has said that blindness has been a great gift for her spiritual and creative growth. Her presence on this earth literally inspires people.

Suffering can lead you to the realms of inner courage. If everything in the outer world always went beautifully, would you ever go within? It has been said that, when we experience suffering and hardship, we turn to God and our spiritual path. I have often witnessed this truth with my AIDS and cancer patients. Despite being ravaged by the disease, many acquire a palpable serenity and tranquility.

Teachers

These same principles of gratitude apply to experiencing appreciation for the significant teachers in your life, whether they are parents, friends, instructors, professors, therapists, counselors, elders, or clergy. Expressing gratitude for their precious gifts of wisdom, support, and guidance increases the benefits you have received.

Benefits of Focusing on Gratitude

In summary, when you focus on what you are grateful for:

- You disconnect from misery and suffering, viewing your life from a different perspective.

- You experience again what you are grateful for.

- You are more receptive to the blessings in your life under the current circumstances.

- You have an increased experience of the grace present in your life. Life becomes more pleasurable and joyous.

Spiritual practices such as chanting, prayer, and meditation also attract grace by increasing your reservoir of spiritual energy. The more you raise your vibration yourself, creating a humble, grateful heart, the more that grace will follow you.

How Gratitude Draws Grace Into Your Life: Written Contemplation

List whatever you feel grateful for in the following areas. Find specific, enjoyable ways to express your gratitude (such as ceremonies, letters, meals, hugs, and so forth).

Your Body:

The Earth:

Your Home:

Your Finances:

Your Friendships:

Your Job:

Teachers in Your Life:

Opportunities for Growth:

Gratitude, like selfless service, has the attributes of a spiritual practice. Gratitude invites you to receive benefits from whatever life is offering. What could be better than that?

7

The Secrets of Prosperity

What does prosperity mean to you?

Prosperity is not an outer set of circumstances. It is an inner state of mind, a higher level of consciousness. It is the experience of having more than enough in this moment to meet your needs. As a result, there is a consciousness of sharing from a state of fullness instead of from a state of scarcity. Is your cup half-full or half empty? Focusing on the cup being half-full, you begin tasting the abundance that is present in the now.

In the 1980s, Robin Leach made us aware of *Lifestyles of the Rich and Famous*. We vicariously watched people spend large sums of money on clothing, fancy cars, homes, and vacations. I have personally been amazed that, after a period of lavish spending, some of my clients have an abrupt shift. Suddenly, the mind-set of "I have all the money in the world!" and "I can fly to Bali to buy exotic furniture and then ski in St. Moritz this winter!" becomes "I can only buy clothes on sale." and "I can't afford to go out for dinner anymore." Playing witness to this extreme dance of spending/not spending, I saw that prosperity is not about money. It is a state of being. Perhaps they did spend extravagantly on themselves or gifts for others. Perhaps it is frivolous to go on spending sprees. Perhaps some of these people feel guilty for such indulgences. However, none of this really matters.

What matters is that people who approach prosperity from this point of view unwittingly limit themselves. For them, prosperity is about money. There is nothing intrinsically wrong or unspiritual about money. Without a question, money can make many aspects of life easier, but it is just a small part of true prosperity.

One way I have experienced prosperity is from the many blessings I have received during my travels. Friends and strangers have made their homes or guesthouses available for me to stay in and for doing my sessions. I deeply appreciate these acts of generosity. Some of these hosts literally had no money coming in, yet they graciously offered their homes to share with me. The spirit of generosity flooded their hearts, and they are now experiencing great abundance. This is true prosperity.

Six Elements of Prosperity

Prosperity is not something that arrives on your doorstep in a neat package. It is something to practice in thought, word, and deed. There are six elements of prosperity: gratitude, outflow, selfless service, releasing, conservation, and alignment to *dharma*. Each contributes a special aspect to your overall experience of prosperity. All should be part of your daily life.

1. Gratitude

Gratitude is a sublime practice. As you accept and embrace what you have, a remarkable opening occurs. You are more present and connected to everyone and everything in your environment. Serenity replaces struggle. A sense of the perfection of this moment, in these circumstances, becomes evident. The deeper the gratitude for simple essential aspects of life (shelter, home, food, family, friends, community, the arts, nature, spirituality), the freer you are to reap the benefits. Life is so different life when you experience gratitude as a vehicle for your enlightenment. (See chapter 6.) A great practice is to experience gratitude for everything in your life, even the challenges.

2. Outflow

Consistent outflow shifts your attention from "I want! I need!" to "What can I contribute?" Outflow does not need to be dramatic or grandiose. In fact, because outflow does not need to be about material goods at all, it can become a constant, organic aspect of daily living. For example, in our frenetic society, we too rarely slow down and give others the gift of our full attention. Notice how you feel when someone takes the time and energy to really be there for you. This sort of outflow is literally priceless. You might practice outflow by taking the time to write or call someone as your expression of love and concern. The gift of time and attention is extremely valuable and not to be taken for granted.

Of course, outflow may also be expressed by giving money to your family, friends, charities, and good causes. Tithing is the spiritual practice of contributing one-tenth of your income to the organization from which you receive spiritual support. The word tithe means to give one-tenth. To me, consistent outflow in the world is more important than tithing.

A generous spirit attracts prosperity. One friend of mine is a very ample tipper at restaurants and car washes as well as toward people who provide her with various services. She gives gifts or meals to friends and family as she takes great care of herself. Because of her consistent outflow, she experiences great good fortune in her life and is living validation of the power of outflow.

Try this way of connecting to life around you. If you cannot give money or gifts, offer smiles, hellos, interest, and appreciation. Your environment will soon feel like a little bit of paradise.

3.   Selfless Service

Serving others selflessly without attachment to rewards or reciprocation is in itself a spiritual practice In Sanskrit, this is called *seva* (pronounced say-vah) and is at the heart of all religious and humanitarian teachings. In the *Bhagavad-Gita*, it says, "Renounce the fruits of your actions." It is your duty, your *dharma*, to perform good actions and then let them go.

When you open your heart and mind to be of service to others, you also experience great benefits for yourself. Selfless service temporarily takes your focus off your own challenges and drama. Without obsessing on them, your problems will begin to resolve themselves. As the saying goes, "God takes care of those who serve others." During periods of financial hardships and unemployment, some clients of mine volunteered for organizations or causes they believed in. In no time, they acquired new friends and career opportunities and experienced a considerable lessening of their fears and anxieties. This is the grace that comes from *seva*, taking the focus off your ego self and placing it on serving others. I am convinced my mother's *seva* in the nursing homes all of these years is the source of her great vitality, even into her late eighties.

We sometimes feel too exhausted to serve. At times, I have not wanted to be there for clients and friends. When this resistance occurs, it is usually a sign I need to recharge my energy. If I choose to assist others while feeling depleted, my inner martyr can easily take over. I give out of sacrifice, not choice. It is never satisfying to act out of some idealized concept of what serving others should look like. Not giving from my heart feels hollow and unfulfilling. During these times, I step back and renew myself. Then, feeling revitalized, I emerge better able to focus on others again.

4. Release

One frequent obstruction to experiencing prosperity is the "c" word. Clutter! Is your home or office jam-packed with boxes, newspapers, letters, magazines, clothes, and other stuff? If so, you may have difficulty releasing things. Refraining from throwing out, giving away, or selling material things that hinder you creates a scarcity consciousness. You may fear that letting go of what you have will leave you with nothing. You may fear allowing something new into your life. Perhaps you fear the unknown will be unpleasant in some way. Change often feels risky, but it is an inevitable part of life. Stubbornly resisting it will only cause other problems. You must embrace change and include it in your experience.

In *feng shui*, the Chinese art of placement, it is recommended you always leave space in your closets, drawers, bookcases, as well as inside and on top of your desk. The principle is that this creates room for new blessings, whether material or immaterial, to arrive in your life.

Material goods are not the only sort of clutter that can infest your space. Clutching onto negative relationships also inhibits your prosperity consciousness. Surrounding yourself with negative company and harmful associations diminishes your self-esteem and ability to release negativity. Your energy becomes stuck. If you are in an abusive relationship, whether physical or psychological, it is easy to take on strong feelings of worthlessness. Such relationships wear down body and spirit, contributing to feelings of being trapped and/or afraid to leave. It takes courage to depart from harmful relationships, but, the more you prolong it, the more adversely you will be affected, even by comparatively minor negativity.

During Damienwork sessions, I assist in the release of emotional trauma. Most trauma is due to not having one's basic needs met as a child. Such experiences create an imprint of scarcity in your cells, which manifests in the present as not wanting to let go of what you have, even if it is negative, useless, or ugly. The condition of scarcity requires examination of your core beliefs.

5. Conservation

The polar opposite of release is conservation. This seeming duality exists in prosperity consciousness. As necessary as it is to shed negative thoughts and attachments to scarcity, you must also conserve and increase your life force energy. Everyone has a natural reservoir of life force energy. When we dissipate this source through excessive living, we leak out *shakti*, our spiritual fuel. If a sudden crisis occurs when you have depleted your storehouse of reserve energy, you are more likely to be devastated and crumble from stress.

Moderation is the key. You need not be excessive or austere. You can find the balance in the imbalance. Your most potent investment is to take time to improve the quality of your thoughts and spoken words and acquire a certain amount of self-restraint.

"I am" is the most powerful phrase in the English language. "I am" affirms your oneness with the creative source in the universe. Saying "I am poor" sends a message to your brain and creates your emotional reality. When you shift your declaration to "I have fears of poverty or thoughts of poverty," you acknowledge a distance between yourself and your condition. You are not your fear of poverty. You have your fear of poverty. Try this way of speaking. Notice how it alters your experience.

Obviously, conservation should include saving money as well as refraining from overspending and going into debt. *Dharmic* spending is a spiritual practice requiring moment-by-moment contemplation. Will you choose to purchase that which is tantalizing? "I must have that!" Will you restrain yourself and only purchase that which is beneficial in the long run? From personal experience, I know it is not so easy. It has been a very long, often frustrating process for me to become free of debt. On some days, it looks like it will never happen. As fun as it is to give myself the treats I desire, like Broadway theatre tickets and travel experiences, it is equally essential to save for necessities. What a relief it is to no longer beat myself up for being in debt. Instead, I accept responsibility for the choices I have made.

Debts are bits of Karma to be paid, opening doors to greater abundance. Weekly, set aside money for future needs, including taxes, retirement, gifts, long-term purchases (property, furniture, or a car), short-term purchases (clothes, theatre tickets, and vacations), medical insurance, and paying off existing credit card balances. This practice will support you in moving out of debt or remaining free of debt. Because I have regularly set aside funds for these categories, money has been there for me, and my quality of life has improved.

You can also increase your life force energy through spiritual practices like meditation, chanting, celibacy, Taoist sexual exercises, and Tantra. See what appeals to you. Conserving and increasing your life force energy is like depositing money in the bank of your future Karmic benefits. It is well worth the effort. Why not start today?

6. Alignment to *Dharma*

Dharma is the path of compassionate, truthful living. When your body, relationships, home, career/work choices (that is, your life path) is aligned with your *dharma*, you will experience more synchronicity in the dance of life. Even amidst challenges and difficult lifecycles, prosperity will always be present. Take the focus off the dollars coming in, and put your attention on flowing with life. As you are more in harmony with yourself and your environment, your outer circumstances will support you with greater abundance.

In *dharma*, the elements of gratitude, outflow, selfless service, releasing, and conserving come together. When you experience gratitude and outflow in the spirit of selfless service, your intentions and actions contribute to the world, releasing what is no longer appropriate, thus conserving and increasing your life force. You will enter a state of alignment. Together, these are the six elements of prosperity. Let's discover how to integrate them further.

Scarcity Enquiry: A Contemplation

When you were growing up, was there an experience of scarcity? Did it revolve around money, love, attention, affection, encouragement, pleasure, privacy, or spare time? How did this affect you? What were your family's prevailing beliefs about scarcity?

If your family believed there was never enough to go around, belief in scarcity may have become deeply embedded in your consciousness. Separating yourself from the prevailing scarcity beliefs in your family lineage is essential in order to experience prosperity now. Unless you do the inner work, you may be destined to live out limiting ancestral beliefs and pass them on to future generations.

The Secrets of Prosperity: Written Contemplation

1. In your life, what are you most grateful for? What life conditions are you resisting and complaining about?

2. What would it feel like if you were to express gratitude for your life exactly as it is? What if your life was packed with opportunities to teach you all you need to know to experience greater prosperity?

3. How do you outflow your generous spirit in day-to-day living? How do you selflessly serve others? Where do you withhold your service?

4. Is your home, car, or office a disaster area? Does clutter permeate your life? Do you keep company with negative people? How does that affect you?

5. Are you dissipating your life force through excess overeating, oversexing, overspending, overdrinking, overworking, overtalking, or overworrying? What are the ramifications of this in your life? How can you practice conservation in your life today? If necessary, are you willing to create a new spending plan?

Again, when you experience gratitude and outflow with the spirit of selfless service, your intention and actions contribute to the world, releasing what is no longer appropriate, thus conserving and increasing your life force. You will then enter a state of alignment.

8

How to Change Your Karma in This Lifetime

What is Karma?

Karma is a Sanskrit word that describes the law of cause and effect in the universe. Every cause has an effect. In both Hindu and Buddhist philosophy, the results of all of your thoughts, words, and actions from this and all of your past lives is called your Karma. It is said that every thought, word, and action is recorded in the universe. Positive thoughts, words, and deeds create positive results, while negative thoughts, words, and deeds create negative results. Therefore, each of us can choose what sort of Karma we accumulate.

What are samskaras?

Samskara is a Sanskrit word for the lasting impressions of thoughts, words, and deeds from past lives. Perhaps you do not believe in past lives. If so, perhaps you can accept there is energy in your thoughts now and this energy becomes part of your vibration. It is easy to test this. Try sending loving thoughts to those around you and then notice the effect. They will respond to the energy in your thoughts. When you have experienced many loving thoughts and performed many good actions, your presence radiates love and compassion, whatever you are consciously thinking.

Fearful, judgmental, or hateful thoughts also add to your vibration, but, in this case, people may not feel safe or comfortable around you. Notice the energy emanating from people emerging from a vigilante rally, filled with hate and the call for revenge. Compare this to the energy of a group who has just prayed, chanted, or meditated for peace. The vibrations of each group are distinctly different. In the former, there is hostility and provocative divisiveness. In the latter, there is serenity and expansiveness. *Samskaras* are traces of old emotional states, intentions, and actions lingering in the present. You might think of your *sam-skaras* as a web or shawl around your body. *Samskaras* are not physically percepti-ble, yet the impressions exist.

Besides thoughts, your words become *samskaras*. Words consist of sound vibrations and are alive. Have you ever noticed that words of someone who has practiced great contemplation and purified his or her speech carry great power? You feel you can trust such a person. His or her words uplift you. Personally, I have experienced this in the presence of Gurumayi Chidvilasananda and Vanessa Redgrave. Their actual words and sound vibrations inspired me. Each word struck me as highly alive, charged with energy and intention.

Your previous actions also become *samskaras*. The vibration of someone who has performed honorable actions has an aura of integrity, so you feel safe around such a person. Some people elicit very negative responses from you without utter-ing a word. When they do speak, there is an absence of peace and love. Due to their *samskaras*, you do not feel comfortable around them.

Years ago, I did healing sessions in a Chicago townhouse where two huge col-lies, Dylan and Conrad, lived. One day, an animal rights advocate came for a healing. As always, I put the temporary gate at the foot of the stairs to prevent the collies from intruding on the session, but, precisely at the conclusion of this ses-sion, Conrad leapt over the fence, ran up the stairs, and energetically licked my client's forehead. This was the only time Conrad behaved this way during my time there. I am convinced that animals sense our *samskaras*. They know if you have been kind or cruel to their fellow furry friends and respond in kind.

Karma and *Samskaras* in Action

In the 1990s, a film called *Hero* perfectly demonstrated the laws of Karma and how the choices we make influence both our destiny and the lives of others. In the film, Dustin Hoffman's character witnesses a plane crash and rescues several passengers from the burning wreck. Before then, he led a rather irresponsible, selfish life. Only with resistance did he perform these good deeds. Afterwards, he fled the scene. The public wondered who the mysterious hero was.

In the meantime, a character played by Andy Garcia, who had a reputation performing good deeds, told reporters he was the mysterious hero. After the media made him famous, the public showered him with adulation, fame, awards, and money. Although Hoffman's character tried telling people he was the true hero, no one believed him because of his past behavior. His negative past Karma followed him. Ironically, in this case, the residue of Garcia's character's good

Karma protected him so the public accepted his deception, but I believe the newly created, negative Karma would eventually catch up with him. It may not be immediate, but your good or bad Karma does come looking for you. You can count on this.

At the close of *Hero*, it becomes evident that Hoffman's character is transforming. He rescues a child from a lion at the zoo. His previous good action has already begun transforming him into a more aware, compassionate person. In many ways, Karma is like an insurance policy. Your good actions can protect you both now and in the future, while harmful actions toward yourself or others will attract conflicts and problems. The good news is that it is up to you. Choose wisely!

Why are we here on this earth?

In Sanskrit, the earth is called *Karma Bhumi*, the Land of Karmas. Think of your life on earth as the ultimate in great experiments. You live on this earth to work through all of your Karma, to purify yourself so you live in a state of Buddhahood, becoming the awakened, compassionate one.

How do you work through your Karma?

Face Karma head on. When good Karma (financial boon, great job, splendid relationship, recovery from an illness, profound spiritual awakening, and so forth) occurs, stop, pause, and breathe. Open your heart, and accept what is. Feel any excitement that is present, and connect with your gratitude. Do not dissipate the feeling. Enjoy it. If you claim it, it will settle beneficially in your heart.

When bad Karma occurs, treat it with the same attentive respect. Perhaps you have just had your car stereo stolen. Pause, breathe, open your heart, and accept what is. Do not dissipate your upset. Allow your feelings. They will eventually dissolve into your heart. You are paying off negative Karma. Perhaps, whether in this lifetime or in another, you committed a theft. You are now experiencing the flip side of that experience. As it says in the Bible, "Ye shall reap what ye shall sow." Karma is redressing the balance of things.

While traveling, have you ever been touched by the generosity and hospitality of strangers? Perhaps you were given food, shelter, and vital assistance while visiting a foreign land. In Karmic terms, you are reaping the effects of the generosity you have previously shared. The next time a tourist asks you for directions, remember, "What goes around comes around."

We work through our Karma on earth until we have completed them. Then we can return to earth as a *Bodhisattva*, one dedicated to alleviating suffering and leading others to enlightenment. Eventually, this becomes our only desire, our only purpose.

In the presence of spiritual teachers who vibrate at a very high frequency, it is possible to have some of your Karma instantly burned away. This was my profound experience with the late Karmapa of Tibet and with Swami Muktananda and Swami Chidvilasananda (also known as Gurumayi). Supreme bliss flooded my heart as large chunks of my negativity were destroyed in the fire of their love.

Seven Strategies for Changing Your Karma

1. Right Understanding and Mindfulness

When you adopt right understanding (that is, everything you think, do, or say has consequences), you will choose to live more mindfully. You can witness yourself speaking and performing actions instead of merely going through the motions in life. You can contemplate your thoughts and ideas, determining whether they are serving or harming you. Instead of chatting incessantly, you can pause and reflect on whether what you want to say is appropriate at this time. Instead of exposing yourself to gossip and sensationalism, you can be more selective about what you listen to and read. Because you digest every experience, why imbibe negativity? Instead of indulging in every sensory pleasure available, you can make appropriate, thoughtful choices. When you choose to eat that piece of chocolate, take your time to savor each moment.

Mindful living trains you to be attentive to the needs of the soul. Mundane chores (for example, washing dishes or housekeeping) performed with mindfulness can be energizing experiences. As you understand the importance of each moment, word, action, and encounter, life becomes a heightened adventure to create more positive Karma and a better quality of living.

2. Awareness and Acceptance

To begin changing your Karma, you must first discover what your Karma continues to be. Are you always broke? Do you find it difficult holding on to a job? Are you attracted to people who are physically or emotionally unavailable? Do you feel stuck in your life? Do things seem to be hopeless?

When you examine your current challenges, you need to accept that your thoughts, words, and actions drew this experience to you. You are not being punished. It is not useful or beneficial to riddle yourself with guilt about this. Simply acknowledge that some part of you is attracting this experience. Accepting what is, you can choose to be peaceful and empowered to receive benefit from every situation. Instead of creating unnecessary suffering, why not find the hidden benefit in the situation? Why not learn the lesson so you do not need to repeat it?

3.   Willingness to Change

On a mindful path, it is required that you be impeccably honest. You must contemplate, "Am I truly willing to have my life change for the better?" After all, change does not come easily. It requires courage and persistence. Despite your resistance, life already guarantees change. You are either willing to accept the tides of change or spend your days in a state of perpetual resistance. Your willingness to change opens the door to miracles.

4.   Acts of Reparation

In twelve-step recovery programs, it is said we need to take inventory of our lives, reflecting on and clarifying how we have hurt others. Participants make lists of those who they have harmed and find appropriate ways to make amends (for example, face-to-face meeting, writing a soulful letter, repaying money or returning something loaned).

Years ago, I had an alcoholic roommate who was in an abusive relationship. Living with this was extremely stressful. Once, I even had to bring him to the emergency room. When I reached my limit, I told him I could not tolerate his drinking any longer and moved out. Five years later, he made amends, inviting me to an AA meeting where he declared how his actions had hurt me. Our negative Karma was healed, and we became the best of friends.

Such acts of reparation create a greater space to love yourself and others. These acts require great courage and are extremely beneficial in changing the Karma of future relationships.

5.   Acknowledging Your Bad Habits

As part of your personal inventory, you can contemplate how bad habits impede your progress, remembering it is important to acknowledge your misdeeds without beating yourself up. Contemplate the following questions:

• Where am I lazy in life?

- How do I procrastinate?

- What other negative habits do I have?

- Am I making an effort to create positive change?

- Do I speak my truth?

- Do I gossip and put others down?

- Is my diet serving my health and well-being?

- Is my body getting enough exercise?

- Do I get enough sleep and rest?

- Do I use sleep, food, alcohol, or drugs to escape from problems?

- How do I escape from facing my challenges?

- Do I have a regular spiritual practice? Am I actively working on my spiritual development?

- Do I regularly serve others?

- Do I set appropriate boundaries with others?

- What are my worst habits?

6. Releasing Your Traumas

Along with cultivating good habits, it is essential that you release emotional traumas from the past that prevent you from having a more satisfying life. You may sometimes not be aware of what you are holding onto from the past. Hands-on energy work and bodywork can greatly help. These techniques are neither ends in themselves nor quick fixes. They are vehicles to release trauma and pain from the past.

Will I ever release all of my traumas and be free of them?

I do not believe you will fully release your past traumas in one fell swoop. The process may take years, even decades. The blueprints of your painful experiences or psychic scars may always remain. However, you do have the opportunity to use these scars as opportunities for growth.

Where can I learn more about this?

Barbara Brennan, a former physicist, has written two books, *Hands of Light* and *Light Emerging,* which demonstrate the amazing power of hands-on healing in a very scientific way. Another invaluable book that promotes self-healing is Machaelle Small-Wright's *M.A.P.—Medical Assistance Program.* Following the MAP guidelines, I have experienced powerful healings of chronic conditions. Of course, spiritual practices like chanting and meditation bring your traumas to the surface so you may release and transform them.

7. Overcoming Resistance

Werner Erhard, founder of EST and the Forum, said, "What you resist persists." If you resist particular people and situations, guess what? They, along with other people embodying the qualities that disturb you, will continue appearing until you accept them. Your boss might be compulsively early. You may let this drive you crazy. At your next job, what do you encounter? A boss who is compulsively early. Why not accept this person or the situation's purpose in your life? It is up to you to choose to experience them as a part of your growth process instead of resisting his or her existence. Your resistance may sometimes take the form of saying no to wonderful opportunities. New people and possibilities will start flooding into your life to support change. You may be saying no to them, their activities, and projects, blocking exactly what you need most.

With mindful living, right understanding, awareness, acceptance of where you are right now, willingness to change, performing acts of reparations, acknowledging your bad habits, releasing your traumas, and overcoming resistance, you can change your Karma one moment at a time. If this seems daunting, it may help to think of changing Karma as a journey-oriented, rather than a destination-oriented, process.

How to Change Your Karma in This Lifetime: Written Contemplation

1. Make some notes.

- Write down some words you have said today about yourself, the people in your life, and the world. Did you praise anyone? Did you criticize others or yourself? Did you find faults in others? Write down the words you said.

- When you last went to work, did you think, "I hate this job. I don't wait to do this," or "I love my life and my work. I am looking forward to today"? Did you say something else entirely?

2. Take a moment to sense how each of your thoughts and words influence your experience of living in this world. In the ancient Yogic philosophy of Kashmir Shavism, it is said, "The world is as you see it." In Buddhism, it is said that your outer environment reflects your inner one. Your thoughts and words create your experience. Are you satisfied with the experiences you are having? What would you like more of? What would you like less of?

3. How is the quality of your health today? What have your habits been for the last few weeks regarding diet, exercise, rest, sleep, and alcohol and/or recreational drugs. Take a moment to consider how your recent habits contribute to the state of your health. Are you feeling exuberant and vigorous or lackluster and sluggish? Consider the results if you change some of your habits.

4. What spiritual practices (for example, prayer, meditation, chanting, contemplation, or selfless service) have you performed lately? Sense the reservoir of spiritual energy you are cultivating due to these practices. Notice what happens when there is no spiritual connection in your life.

5. List any situations where you feel resistance and procrastination, for example, paying taxes, going to the DMV to renew your driver's license, or asking your boss for a raise. Are you willing to face this situation now?

6. List any good actions you have performed for others recently.

The good actions you perform are the rent you pay for your time on earth. Do not motivate these actions by a need to get something. This only creates imbalance and egotism. Have faith that good Karma will eventually come to you. Continue to perform good actions for their own sake. Remember not to beat yourself up for making mistakes.

9

How to Move through Difficult Times and Celebrate Life

In such great traditions as Yoga, Buddhism, Judaism, and Christianity, in various ways, it is stated that life on earth is fraught with suffering. Although pain is inevitable, suffering is not. Pain is a warning that something is wrong. This is important, useful information. Inappropriate attachment to people, material things, and emotional states of being causes suffering.

Is it wrong or unspiritual to have attachments?

No, it is not wrong to have attachments. They are a part of the human condition. However, nothing on this earth—your body, job, clothes, possessions, or loved ones—lasts forever. Nothing you may be attached to can last forever.

Every moment here is preparation for death. When death arrives, we must let everything go. If we practice letting go of our attachments to outer results and life experiences now, it will be easier to let go when we make our transition from this life. There is great growth when we release our attachments, moment by moment.

None of us is immune to suffering. A distraught woman appeared before the Buddha. She was grief-stricken with her dead child limp in her arms. "Please bring my child back to life," she pleaded. The Buddha gazed into her eyes. "I will grant your request if you bring me a mustard seed from a house that has never known death." The woman eagerly set out to comply, covering a vast distance. Walking door to door and from village to village, the same response met her. "Death has touched our family. Yes, death has touched this house." Returning to the Buddha, the woman shared her experience and accepted the Buddha's teaching. She became one of the Buddha's greatest disciples.

No one is immune from suffering on this earth. Everyone experiences losses in this life, whether the loss of a loved one, our health, a job, a home, or a friendship. As humans, our loss can turn into suffering. Our suffering can lead us to our greatest enlightenment.

The Great Fallacy

Perhaps the greatest fallacy is a belief that everything goes smoothly and works perfectly for some people. For them, trains and planes arrive on time. They are free of financial worries, are in perfect health, and have either a perfect mate or a bevy of beautiful lovers waiting for them. In other words, they do not have any big problems. They are so together, and they are always happy. We envy their good fortune.

A very tiny minority of people on the planet do experience inner peace most of the time. This does not mean their cars do not break down or elevators are not stuck in their universe. Instead of resisting unpleasant circumstances, they accept and move through, doing what can be done and releasing everything else. When you believe everything goes well for others (for example, spiritual leaders, celebrities, wealthy people, or beautiful people), it is easy to berate yourself for not being perfect. Constantly comparing yourself to others will destroy your peace of mind. It is a form of resistance to who you are. If you catch yourself in this mind-set, stop, breathe, and remember that things do not go perfectly for anyone. We are all subject to the physical laws of the universe. Some of the greatest gurus have had diabetes and heart attacks. The Dalai Lama wears glasses!

How People React to Difficulties

After much observation, I have noticed that people respond in three basic ways to challenges, conflicts, and crises.

1. The Overcontroller

The overcontroller becomes obsessed with controlling everyone and everything around him. He wants things to only go his way. He is tense, distrusting, fearful, and in a state of watchful resistance. He fears everything will crumble if he relinquishes control even for an instant. This failure would be too humiliating to bear.

2. The Retreater

Another tactic is retreating. When the going gets tough, leave! Do not face your fears or challenges. The retreater avoids them. He stays home and does not pick up the phone or check e-mail. He may sleep all day to escape from the world outside. Because he does not communicate, he cannot ask for support. He is very isolated.

Perhaps, when a crisis erupts, it is all right to retreat for a day or so, but extended retreat can—and will—work against you. After acting out the retreater in my own life, I have humbly learned I cannot escape from any of my problems. The same issues have followed me year after year, in every city where I have lived or worked.

3. The Out-of-Controller

Yet another common response to crises and challenges is to freak out and lose control, crying, shaking, ranting, and raving. By being dramatically unable to function, the out-of-controller indicates he wants to be rescued. "Help me!" he cries.

Although it is sometimes necessary to let go of control in order to accept our limitations, this strategy can be abused if it is employed as a means of escaping responsibility. The out-of-controller's unwillingness to face a challenge is very different from surrendering to what is and acknowledging there is only so much you can do for now. This sort of surrender leads to a state of deep listening, discovery, and a sort of relief, but the out-of-controller will never find peace. He is stuck in his resistance.

The Reality of Outer Circumstances

Life provides us with cycles when we may contract a serious illness, have a debilitating injury, face the death of a loved one, or experience financial hardship. In the midst of it all, remind yourself that it is only a cycle, not your eternal lot in life. Life guarantees change. You may be feeling terrific about your life and then develop a throbbing headache or nauseating stomachache. It can be challenging to not allow these maladies to destroy your peace of mind. Have you ever found it tempting to use aches and pains as an excuse not to be kind to others or yourself? One of my practices is grounding myself and keeping my heart open, attempting to be very present and aware of others, even if I am not feeling well. Often, some of my physical or emotional pain dissipates during this process.

Alternatively, have you ever had favorable, delightful circumstances for you personally, yet not for your closest family and friends? A loved one may be ill. Your mate may be angry with you. A friend may need you in a crisis. How do you handle this imbalance?

The pleasure of your good fortune is sometimes abruptly dismantled. Your environment might be very disruptive. I have experienced neighbors partying loudly for hours on end and construction workers drilling across the street eight hours a day for months. When you cannot hear yourself think, it is tempting to angrily protest, "How dare they destroy my peace of mind!"

Acts of nature like earthquakes, floods, tornadoes, and snowstorms can stop ordinary life in its tracks. It could be very easy to delay creating well-being in the now. "I have five feet of snow to shovel from my driveway." "The plumbing isn't working since the earthquake." "I have no home to return to after the flood." In the future, there will be weather and calamities for us to face. What's a human being to do?

Violence, whether natural or human, can strike without warning. I lived in New York City during both of the World Trade Center attacks. It would have been easy and understandable to lose all peace of mind afterwards. However, particularly after the 9/11 attack, the city became surprisingly quiet, even peaceful. New Yorkers slowed down and took the time to connect with each other on the street. Cars stopped honking. Shrines were all over the city. Every time I took a walk, I was moved to tears.

I have weathered the stock market crashing and the dot coms collapsing. Many of my clients were suddenly unemployed or had their income cut in half. While some abruptly canceled all of their sessions with me, others came less frequently. I could have let this devastate me, but I did not. Even when disaster strikes, you can go on.

Seven Steps to Rising above Circumstances

You must be willing to find courage within in order to rise above your external circumstances. This requires your intention, perseverance, and willingness to succeed. I have found that seven steps are necessary to rise above surprises, crises, and challenging circumstances. Following them will support you in celebrating your life once again.

1. Ask for Grace, Spiritual Support, and Protection

When things are not going well for you and problems abound, stop. Take some deep breaths. Ask for grace. Invoke spiritual support through chanting, meditation, or prayer. Alternatively, bring yourself to stillness for a few minutes. Breathing in a relaxed, conscious manner, then draw your spiritual support into your body. This simple practice can produce powerful change.

Boarding a train from Long Beach to downtown Los Angeles as always, I invoked protection. The guru Swami Muktananda appeared to me. I immediately heard these words, "You are going to be all right. Become completely still and chant." I quietly began chanting one of my mantras. As we approached Watts, I noticed I was the only Caucasian on the train. In the next instant, I heard screams as a gunshot roared through the crowded train. Someone had shot at me from outside, and part of the window was shattered. Thankfully, I was safe. Before each challenge on my path, I gratefully chant and ask for protection. I encourage you to do this as well.

2. Accept the Situation as It Is

What if things are truly horrific? Suppose you are dealing with calamity, death, disease, war, destruction, and the worst possible circumstances. First, accept the situation as it is. You cannot move ahead until you do this. Even in the worst possible scenario, it is possible to accept what is and then move forward with courage and peace, even in solitary confinement.

St. John of the Cross was imprisoned in a tiny cell without any light or space to move about. A miniscule opening was provided for bread and water once a day. The church was punishing him for performing certain activities without permission. In such an environment, St. John entered an ecstatic state and composed some of the most beautiful spiritual poetry—all in his head. There was no pen or paper available to him. One day, the jailer sensed something special emanating from St. John's cell and knew he was in the presence of a great, joyous being. Living in virtual hell, St. John transcended his outer circumstances and created something beautiful. The jailer helped him escape.

St. John's story proves—even in the worst possible environments (prisons, shelters, concentration camps, and so forth)—it is possible to transform the experience of suffering. That journey begins by accepting what is.

3. Contemplate: What is the Opportunity Here?

Stand back, breathe, and consider what lesson is being presented. How can you grow through this challenge? Dealing with an illness may be an opportunity to change your lifestyle so the body can repair and renew itself to extend your life. Grieving the loss of a loved one can signal the opportunity to receive greater love and support. The loss may actually expand your connection to the community and help you find your true tribe where you feel seen and strengthened. Foundering in debt is an opportunity to transform your relationship with money and spending. By dealing with this problem, you can create a more secure future based on your actions in the now.

Every crisis holds an opportunity for transformation if you are open to the possibility. Facing your life crises and challenges helps clear negative Karma from the past. Chunks of old, negative energy are burned away as we become more courageous, clearing the way for peace of mind.

4. Determining Your *Dharma*

Contemplate the right action for this challenging situation. Is it making a phone call, sending an e-mail, saying a prayer, writing a letter, paying someone a visit, sending a gift, or confronting your discomfort? Ask, "What is my *dharma*, or duty, in this situation?" If you listen, it will be revealed to you. It is sometimes our *dharma* to do very little in the outer world but be quiet and intensely focused within. During other times, we may be called to assertively take charge of the situation.

During health crises in my family, I have learned I can make a difference by sending long-distance healing energy and chanting for others, even if they are thousands of miles away. Sometimes, while visiting relatives or friends, it has been my *dharma* to offer them healing treatments. During other times, it has been my *dharma* to find peace within and contribute my state of well-being to everyone around me. I have been tested many times (including during my father, brother, and niece's fatal illnesses). Fulfilling my individual *dharma*, feelings of separation and anxiety were dispelled. At the time, it felt like a miracle.

5. Find a Support Person

It can be tempting either to talk obsessively about a disturbing crisis or challenge or to withdraw. Both strategies have pitfalls. Some will immediately call friend after friend after friend, but repeatedly dredging up your story may leave you feeling disturbed and depleted. On the other hand, if you do not want to speak to anyone because you feel you need not—or should not—share your problems, fears, and upsets, the self-imposed isolation can leave you feeling too overwhelmed to act. As always, balance is the key.

Find a support person you can check in with. Choose someone who will lend a nonjudgmental ear. This person does not need to be a therapist or counselor. It could simply be a trusted friend. Throughout the years, I have been blessed with friends who provided this kind of support.

6. Take Great Care of Yourself

Have you ever noticed, when things are not going well, you stop taking care of yourself at the most basic levels? You either stop eating altogether or overindulging. You may eliminate nutritious choices and dive right into your favorite junk food. You reach for a cigarette or drink and go straight into addictive behavior. If this is your pattern, then understand you are acting out of fear. Instead, choose to immediately stop your inappropriate behavior. This is crucial because, if you do not take care of your body, how can you possibly have the stamina required to face difficult circumstances?

The same applies to sleep and exercise. No matter what, take care of the basics. Promise yourself this. Take great care of yourself. Eat well, get enough sleep, and exercise regularly. Do not let your life circumstances create a detour from the source of your physical strength.

7. Perform Good Actions as an Offering to the Highest

Now that you have invoked spiritual and emotional support, accepted what is, contemplated the opportunity available, discovered your *dharma* in the situation, and are taking care of yourself, it is time to perform your *dharmic* actions.

Sometimes, if you do not like the person or persons involved, you can perform your actions to their Buddha Nature/Christ Self/Higher Self instead of their personality. You do not need to like people in order to serve them. Find something positive within everyone to focus on, or serve him or her as an offering to God, the universe, or humanity.

Life may call on you to wash soiled underwear or bathe a smelly, ugly body. These are perfect vehicles to alter your perception and offer your actions to the highest forms in the universe. Before you know it, your ego stops running the show, and grace floods your heart. When Mother Theresa was asked how she could tend to those with leprosy in the most miserable human conditions, she responded, "As I look into their eyes, I see Christ in disguise." I have found, during challenging times (for example, train or plane delays), it helps to just connect with people around me. During one seven-hour delay in Bologna, Italy, I bonded with two British gentlemen. We had dinner, beer, and jovial conversation. It was a pleasant way to pass the time instead of miserably complaining.

Life is not always pleasant. When you use disturbing outer circumstances to go deeper and find your inner courage and vitality, life becomes a cause for celebration!

How to Move through Difficult Times and Celebrate Life: Contemplation

Let's take another look at how you handle your life when things are not going well or when your life is in a state of crisis. As you take yourself through this exercise, apply this to a recent crisis/challenge to see how you responded. Alternatively, apply this to a current challenge to see how you are handling it. Do you become the overcontroller, retreater, or out-of-controller?

New Strategies

1. Stop everything. Become very still. If possible, do not blink. Gaze a few feet in front of you with relaxed eyes. Breathe evenly for a few minutes. Let your mind be quiet. Ask for spiritual support. Chant or pray to connect to your spiritual power. Acknowledge you are not alone. Your higher power is always with you.

2. Accept the situation as it is. Of course, you would prefer things to be different. Step back. Observe the situation as if you are viewing a movie. Make peace with what is.

3. Contemplate the following: What is the opportunity here? Is it to be more courageous, more loving, more compassionate, or more assertive? How can you use this as an opportunity to experience greater aliveness?

4. Contemplate the following: What is my *dharma*? What are you called to do? How can you make a positive contribution in this situation? How can you serve those involved? What actions can you take?

5. Find a support person. Find someone you trust who will be there for you in a loving, nonjudgmental way. Find someone you may share your deepest fears with. Make sure they agree to be there as your support person. You cannot simply assign this role.

6. Take great care of yourself. Pay attention to the basics. Make sure you are getting enough rest, eating nutritious food, and exercising regularly. Limit alcohol, caffeine, and sugar. Regardless of how much you may want to sacrifice your well-being for the situation, don't. Be there first for yourself and then respond to the situation.

7. Perform good actions as an offering to the highest. Take a few deep breaths. Now that you are aware of what you need to do, offer those actions to the highest forces of love and light within the people involved and the universe. Put intention into your actions so they will greatly benefit others. Let go of the need for approval or acknowledgement for your actions. Simply perform these actions as an offering from your heart.

Find the courage within to rise above your life circumstances.

10

Sharing Your Heart of Compassion

Compassion is considered the essential teaching in both Yoga and Buddhism. The Latin root of the English word compassion is "com," meaning "together." "Pati' means "to suffer." So, "compassion" means to "come together with suffering." The Sanskrit word for compassion is *daya*. Most commonly, compassion refers to an unselfish awareness of another's pain, but compassion also needs to be directed toward your own struggling and imperfections. This necessitates pausing, standing back, and recalling how you have been challenged and have suffered but continue to move forward while living your truth.

What did the Buddha mean when he said, "Life is suffering"?

Obviously, great joy is inherent in life. However, in every experience of joy, there is also an element of suffering. Consider that each beginning also marks an ending. At traditional Jewish weddings, for example, the groom stomps on a glass to symbolize the remembrance of the suffering that is always present in life, even on the merriest occasions. So-called mixed emotions are common. Sometimes, you can love so much that it is painful. Perhaps you are thrilled to receive your dream job, but you feel very sad because you have to move to another state. When there is joy, there may be loss.

In suffering, there is also an element of joy. Part of you is observing your emotion or suffering, but it does not touch you. Your Buddha Nature, your peaceful, spiritual awareness, is very present during your suffering. This part of you knows you are connected to the perfect order of the universe and unconditional love, regardless of what is transpiring in your life. Let's share the higher nature we all possess by performing compassionate actions for others and ourselves.

The Value of Performing Compassionate Actions

Performing compassionate actions for yourself is self-love in action. Feeding your body nourishing foods, exercising, resting and/or sleeping enough, maintaining a spiritual practice, sharing your creative gifts, taking care of yourself financially, spending time with nature, playing, laughing, learning, and exploring are expressions of compassion in action. Obviously, this same principle applies toward others. Outflowing compassionate action is how you exercise and strengthen your compassion muscles. Really listening to others, assisting, sending smiles and blessings, and outflowing your energy generously also work out your compassion muscles. Compassion is a spiritual practice requiring courage and fortitude. Have you ever noticed how challenging it is to be compassionate toward those you intensely dislike?

You can choose to make performing compassionate actions a daily priority. Through this practice, you burn away some of your heaviest Karma. Fortunately, you can forget about doing this perfectly. You will inevitably make mistakes, but your intention and inner state are even more important than the actions themselves. When I studied catechism in 1979 to learn the Roman Catholic tradition, my Franciscan teacher said, "The only difference between a sinner and a saint is that a sinner keeps falling down, falling down, falling down. A saint keeps falling down, keeps falling down, keeps falling down, and then picks himself back up. This religion is not about being perfect. It is about the amount of love you have in your heart." I engraved these words that Father Blais spoke in my heart.

Words/Thoughts/Actions/*Dharma*

As discussed in chapter 8, every moment on your spiritual path is precious. Every second of your life, you have a positive or negative influence on your environment. All of your thoughts are very powerful. When you catch yourself slipping into limited, destructive thinking, you do not need to stay there. You can stop, breathe, and think of something life-affirming or repeat your mantra. You can contemplate your words before you speak. As each urge to speak or act emerges, you are free to decide if this will lead to unity or divisiveness. If your impulse is not compassionate, you can witness it and let it dissolve instead of making it manifest. Every day, you can affirm your intention to perform compassionate actions, aligning with your *dharma* moment by moment.

The Media

As a society, the media profoundly affects us. We will sit in front of the television, glued to a scandalous trial for hours or watch as a horrific event is broadcast repeatedly. Many watch or listen to the news first thing in the morning and last thing in the evening, regularly allowing our senses to be bombarded with scandals, gossip, calamities, and disasters. When we give a large amount of time to the media, we also give it our power. Because everything you read and see affects you, do you really want to steep yourself in trauma and suffering?

In order to be on a spiritual path, does this mean you must forgo all media coverage, including the television news, magazines, and newspapers?

You should not put your head in the sand like an ostrich, but you can decide when and how to learn what's happening in the world. In my experience, the media attempts to control society's values, opinions, beliefs, and, most obviously, spending. The media constantly creates and promotes fear, hypnotizing the masses regarding terrorism, crime, weather, and state of the economy. It is important to retain your free will and not give your power to the media.

Part of being on a spiritual path is acknowledging you are an individual. You do not allow yourself to be programmed by others. You have your own opinions and identity. Some seekers choose to not watch television, Internet, or radio new coverage. Instead, they select newspapers and magazines they feel deal honestly with issues. Refraining from twice-daily doses of news frees up a considerable amount of time. You might use some of it to perform good actions for your family, friends, and community or spiritual practices like chanting or meditation to raise your vibration.

Media Strategy Exercise

Excessive exposure to news media can be a negative on the spiritual path. Stop watching the news or reading newspapers for a week. Notice how you feel about your world. Instead of resuming your habit, experiment with the amount of media stimulation in your life until you find a comfortable, appropriate balance.

Downtime

In order to support compassionate living, we need some downtime when neither deep contemplation nor work activities are required. That is, give yourself time for chilling out. As I travel around the nation spending time with people for several hours a day, I also need a break. Selective television watching can be restorative. I enjoy some television dramas and comedies, but I avoid extremely violent or sensational shows. I sometimes gravitate toward educational or musical programs on PBS, Bravo, the History Channel, or A&E. Renting DVDs can be pleasurable. For some, watching sports events provides great relaxation.

There needs to be space for passive relaxation in our lives. Television can fill that need as long as you select the content mindfully. Others find that reading, sewing, or just drinking a cup of tea in a garden setting is quite restorative.

The People in Our Lives

The temptation sometimes arises to shirk responsibility and indulge whims. "I'm there too much for other people," our egos roar. "All I do is give, give, give!" Perhaps this is true. Maybe you are overly identifying with the archetype of the caregiver. Hiding behind that role can enable you to avoid taking care of your own needs. I have learned to stop for a few minutes when I am in this state and do something nurturing to take care of myself, even if it is just drinking a glass of water before I resume my activities. When you feel good about taking care of yourself, the next progression is wanting to relate to others and help alleviate suffering in your environment. Your family, friends, and coworkers are the perfect relationships in which to practice compassionate living. As you practice being completely present for whoever you are with, you can momentarily set your own problems, resentments, and issues aside. You can slow down, listen, and give the gift of your full attention.

There are those passionately committed to serving humanity, yet forget about being of service to their own families and friends. You do not need to go to a third world country or do something dramatic to make a difference. Everything you need to experience for your growth is right in your own backyard. Begin by treating family, friends, coworkers, and neighbors with love and respect as you take great care of yourself. Your buttons will sometimes get pushed. When they do, breathe and acknowledge, "I'm stretching my compassion muscles!"

Selfless Service

The purpose of selfless service is to practice compassion in action without any desire for personal gain. This begins to purify your ego. You do not need to walk around, saying, "I honor you" or bowing and placing your hands together in front of your heart or third eye, as is the custom in the Far East. Your actions say, "I honor you" to another person more loudly than words.

Honoring one another is well-integrated into Asian cultures. It requires temporarily placing your own concerns and agendas aside as you focus openheartedly on whomever you are with. It does not matter how you personally feel about the person. You may even dislike him. The greatest gift you can offer another is your full attention with a compassionate heart. When you are in a higher vibration, your presence makes a positive difference in your environment.

Heart Center Exercise

When you focus on your heart center, you can send positive, loving energy to others. Try silently blessing people as you take a walk while keeping your heart open. Notice how you feel. How do others react? Nothing dramatic may happen, but you will feel better. Focusing energy emanating from your heart transcends the drama of your past. You will be immediately transported to the now. All power for positive change in the world is in the moment, the now.

Years ago, I enrolled in a seminar created by Werner Erhard, entitled, "The Hunger Project: Creating the Context to Eliminate Starvation on the Planet." I loved that seminar. My favorite assignment was serving a person or organization selflessly for two hours. Surrendering to the universe, I asked to be led to the appropriate situation. I was led to a Laundromat on San Francisco's Polk Street. There he stood, a tall Native American with long, black hair, soiled jeans, torn T-shirt, fresh cuts on his face, a black eye, and reeking from alcohol. "Hey, got a cigarette?" he asked. I felt intimidated, but I was there to serve, not judge him. I decided I would accept this challenge, buying him cigarettes and coffee from the corner store. Once I returned, all I did was be present and listen to him. Surprisingly, the longer I focused on him, the more beautiful he became. He shared his life story. After enduring much abuse as a child, he became a prizefighter, struggled with alcoholism, and ended up homeless. After sharing his story, tears streamed down his cheeks. "No one has ever really listened to me," he said. Kissing me on the cheek, he literally lifted me in the air, declaring, "I love you!"

Every time you perform a *dharmic* action from the heart without attachment to outer approval or reward, some of your selfishness is destroyed. If you are waiting until you have it all together before you serve others, it may take a very long time indeed. Forget about being ready. Just start where you are right now.

Accepting Your Teachers as Human

When you go to a therapist, healer, counselor, or spiritual teacher, the state of consciousness he or she is in while working with you is vital. If he or she is in a high state of vibration, you will receive enormous benefit. However, the counselor does not need to be in that exalted state at all times. There is often a large discrepancy between the inspired state of consciousness during a session and the offstage life state, so to speak. Like you, if your counselor waits until reaching perfection, he may never serve others. Instead of seeking or expecting a perfect person, separate the teacher from the teaching, and receive the value that is offered.

Why can't we give our teachers and ourselves permission to be human? Why do we shoot them down for their shortcomings?

Although we know our teachers are human, it is easy to forget this. Instead, we see them as embodied ideals. If they reveal a human shortcoming, the ideal is easily shattered. The teacher is then no longer separate from us. We may feel he is not fit to teach if he has not mastered what he is teaching. Alternatively, we may feel discouraged. If the teacher can make mistakes, what chance of success do we have?

Underlying these issues is self-rejection. If you truly accept your own humanity, then you will also accept your teacher's. Even the greatest teachers, who mirror our Buddha Nature or higher nature, are still human. The reality is that teachers and students possess both aspects to some degree.

Separating the teacher from the teaching can help you be more forgiving of yourself when you fall short of the mark. Duality is part of the human experience. It is as if we have one foot on earth and one foot in heaven. If you cannot allow your teachers to have all of their imperfect humanity, then you will deny this to yourself as well. While being aware of your human imperfections, you can embrace your higher self. Consequently, the quality of your life will improve. Life becomes a joyous adventure, and you are up to the challenge.

Sharing Your Heart of Compassion: Written Contemplation

1.   When do you feel you have truly served others selflessly?

2.   Have you ever served the following selflessly? Friends? Family? Animals? Nature? Your workplace? At church, temple, or place of worship? Your community? Humanity via a cause? If so, what was the experience like for you?

3.   How can you help to alleviate suffering in the world? What is your vehicle for doing this? Are you willing to do this? Set a plan. Remember, it does not need to be grandiose. What can you do to raise your vibration and contribute to the world?

11

Release, Renewal, and the Power of Ritual

Everything in life is cyclical. With every new experience, life offers you the opportunity to release your negative or inappropriate attachments to the past. Renewing yourself, you are refreshed and receptive to new possibilities. Rituals can support you in releasing and renewing, empowering your experience of moment-by-moment living. They remind you that you are part of the rhythm of eternity.

Initiation

In ancient times, spiritual seekers would journey to a monastery or ashram to receive spiritual initiation from a master. These monasteries and ashrams were usually deeply secluded from society. Venturing along mountain paths or journeying deep into jungles or forests to find the teacher or guru was an important part of the process. Traditionally, the master would have the seeker immerse himself in selfless service, or *seva*, done mindfully as an offering to the highest. Disciples were assigned jobs in the kitchen or garden. This included planting, raking leaves, cleaning, cooking, and performing manual labor. All this was performed to heighten spiritual awareness during mundane activities.

The master's touch, spoken word, look or merely intention bestowed spiritual initiation upon the seeker. The seeker was often presented with a talisman (for example, a necklace, crystal, or article of clothing) imbued with the master's *shakti*. The master would eventually provide the disciple with a mantra, or set of syllables charged with *shakti*, which was to be chanted. In the form of mantra, the master's spiritual energy flowed into the seeker's body. The seeker often had profound spiritual experiences and visions that encouraged him to go deeper in his *sadhana*, that is, his spiritual discipline or path.

In modern times, spiritual seekers do not have to withdraw from society to receive spiritual initiation. Today, the masters often travel, bringing their teaching to a wide audience. I have received spiritual initiation in Tibetan and Yoga traditions from teachers from Dharmasala and India. Thousands attended these programs, which were held in theatres, auditoriums, and even hotel ballrooms. People of all ages and lifestyles gathered to participate in these profound events.

It has delighted me to learn that you can have family and job responsibilities but make substantial spiritual progress. The ancient ideal of total withdrawal from society to pursue a spiritual quest is no longer necessary. In fact, it is not always desirable to separate yourself from the physical demands and routines of your life. If carried out with the right attitude, paying the rent or mortgage, tucking your children to bed at night, and performing your duties can all support your *sadhana*.

What is your path? Listen to your heart. Are you drawn to Yoga, Hinduism, Buddhism, Taoism, Judaism, Islam, Christianity, Native American teachings, or Wicca? Explore. Ask the universe for the right spiritual teacher to appear, and he or she will.

Weddings

The ritual of marriage celebrates the union of two people as they publicly commit to share their lives with mutual love and respect. The theatrical witnessing of this event by family and friends joins everyone in the sacredness of the ceremony. All are exposed to the eternal mystery of relationships. On a deeper level, marriage is the union of yin and yang, the Chinese name for the feminine and the masculine principles. Both principles exist in all of our relationships. Whether between a man and woman or between members of the same sex, the dance of the male and female energy is very present, and marriage celebrates this dance.

Funerals and Memorials

Funerals and memorials are designed for the deceased's family and friends to contemplate their own physical mortality along with the deceased's role in their lives. Various issues are confronted. "Did I express all I needed to say to this person? Is anything left unresolved here? Have I forgiven myself or the deceased for any harmful words and actions? What do I want to remember this person for?" It is an opportunity to experience deep feelings, opening your heart to forgiveness for everything. You may eventually let go of attachment to the person, accepting that he or she has made the transition.

The reality of your own inevitable, physical death is also confronted. Many choose to not deal with the feelings stirred up here. While death is a transition, not an ending, the issue of physical death must be addressed. Funerals and memorials remind you of the sacredness of the present moment in all relationships. Before drifting off to sleep nightly, you can ask yourself, "Did I express my truth today? Did I let people know how much I love them? Did I say yes to life and its boundless opportunities?"

Graduation

Graduations are rites of passage that acknowledge a student's completion of his or her studies. The high school and college graduate receives acceptance and responsibility in the adult community, and it is time to set goals. The end of one phase and beginning of another can be a bittersweet experience, calling for compassion. Because graduations are markers of time, they prompt us to face the fact we are getting older. Even if your childhood was filled with trauma, a part of you may not want to let it go. Graduations provide fresh opportunities to release your previous experience, redefine yourself, and face new challenges.

Seasons

As seasons change, it is a useful to perform rituals aligning ourselves with the cycles of nature. Spring represents renewal. The vernal equinox, the official dawning of spring, usually falls on March 21. It is a perfect day to experience rebirth after the darkness of winter. During spring, we can cultivate our inner gardens. Consider what qualities you would like to cultivate. Perhaps you desire greater patience, humor, and discipline. Create your own ceremony through cooking, baking, painting, dancing, playing music, writing poetry, or storytelling to mark the beginning of your new cycle. You can plant seeds in your outdoor garden, empowering them with love and intention of your new personal goals. Spring is an excellent time to begin a new project. Why not risk expressing yourself more confidently in the world?

Summer solstice, which usually falls on June 21, is when you can reflect on the physical and spiritual seeds you planted in spring. Are they ripening and blossoming? Do they cry out for greater care and pruning? Summer has an expansive, enthusiastic quality, so find rituals to evoke these feelings. In summer, light is abundant, and our skin is more exposed to the sun's warmth. On the summer solstice, rise early like the ancient Druids at Stonehenge, and perform a ceremony to honor and celebrate the outer triumphant sun. On this, the longest day of the year, it is particularly fortuitous to honor the first light of dawn.

The autumnal equinox, which usually falls on September 21, signifies the beginning of harvest. Again, reflect on the seeds you planted and the results they have now produced. Were your actions honorable and performed with the highest integrity? Or have you merely gone through the motions? Are you open to receive good fortune? What are you receiving? Perhaps you have attracted a new friendship or intimate bond. A deeper level of closeness may be developing. Creative projects may be coming to fruition. Honor the harvest in order to celebrate the abundant blessings in our lives. Why not share food in a large gathering with music, art, dancing, and good conversation?

Now, meditate on the inner light on the winter solstice, traditionally occurring on December 21. This is the longest night of the year. In winter, we experience less light in our environments, thus stepping inside our homes to find warmth and sustenance. Instead of focusing on outer accomplishments, realign your relationship with your inner self. Winter is a season of quiet, rest, and reflection. Create your own winter solstice ceremony integrating stillness and contemplation. Review your life until now. You may discover previously hidden patterns and unseen benefits. Lighting a candle or logs in your fireplace can allow the outer light to awaken your inner light. You may choose the following inner dialogue, "What is my purpose? What am I most passionate about in life? What attachments do I need to release in life?"

Happy Birthday to You!

Birthdays symbolize the true beginning of your year. The planetary energies infuse you with creative power. Today, a reflection of the previous twelve months is appropriate. Contemplate your achievements and disappointments. Through self-inquiry, you can discover your goals for the next twelve months. Using visualization, see yourself manifesting your goals.

For my thirty-third birthday, I had an astrologer draw my solar return chart, which reveals exactly where you should be on your birthday to receive the greatest benefit for the coming year. Your location on this special day can have a positive or negative effect on your life in the coming year. I was eager to hear where I would be sent. Would it be Maui, Palm Springs, Venice, or New Orleans? No, it was New Haven, Connecticut, during subzero weather! At the exact time of my birth, I prayed, meditated, and visualized my goals in a large Holiday Inn. Amazingly, I did receive everything I asked for that year.

Anniversaries and New Year's Eve are also beneficial times to perform release/renewal rituals. On New Year's Eve, you can reflect on gains and losses incurred during the passing year. You may begin the new year with a spirit of revelry. During anniversaries, couples can contemplate the different phases of their relationship from courting and commitment through both lean and prosperous times.

Monthly lunar and solar cycles invite ceremonies as well. When the moon is new, it is time to visualize your goals, release the past, and forge new beginnings. The full moon is a time to express your passion through creativity and sharing time with your loved ones.

How to Get Benefits from Solar Cycles

The Sun changes signs approximately every thirty days. Each astrological sign is unique, providing special creative opportunities. The dates I am listing are based on Western or tropical astrology. In Jyotish or Vedic Astrology, each sun sign begins approximately on the fourteenth of the month. The following are brief descriptions of actions and perspectives that are most useful during the period when the sun rises in each astrological sign.

- Aries (approximately March 22 to April 21): Reconnect with the child within. Express your creativity and courage. Find three tasks or actions you have avoided, and complete them.

- Taurus (approximately April 22 to May 20): Consider your relationship to money and the abundance of blessings in your life. Share your prosperity with others. Begin outflowing regularly. Create a financial plan in which you are mindful of saving and spending appropriately.

- Gemini (approximately May 21 to June 19): Declare your appreciation for the diversity of your talents and life experiences as well as the support of partners, both personal and professional. Find someone to work with on a creative project or event. What would you like to manifest together?

- Cancer (approximately June 20 to July 21): Honor the feminine energy and mysteries of the moon. Contemplate your relationship with your mother and the "Mother" energy in the universe. Who are the nurturing women in your life? Actively nurture others by sharing a massage, cooking a meal, drawing a special bath, or fully listening.

- Leo (approximately July 22 to August 22): Perform a ceremony thanking the Sun for its fire that warms your body and home and cooks your food. Contemplate your relationship to your father and the "Father" energy in your life. Who are the nurturing men in your life? Take pleasurable actions expressing your love to others and acknowledging their importance in your life.

- Virgo (approximately August 23 to September 22): Express thanks for the purity in life as well as within yourself, your relationships, and in nature. Refrain from excessive habits that destroy your well-being. Cultivate simplicity.

- Libra (approximately September 23 to October 22): While it is impossible to maintain a state of perfect balance, you may endow your life with harmony, order, and beauty. At the same time, invite greater options for play and spontaneity. Explore beauty wherever you go. How can you create more beauty? How can you see more beauty everywhere?

- Scorpio (approximately October 22 to November 22): Celebrate the mysteries of sex and regeneration. Find ways to honor this profound power. Examine the role of sex in your life. Are you connected to your heart and spirit while making love? Respect sex with Taoist or Tantric sexual practices.

- Capricorn (approximately December 22 to January 19): Perseverance is a major attribute of the spiritual path. Life guarantees interruptions and can be confusing. Despite obstacles, you can forge ahead. Name your top priorities for this month. Stick to your plan while still allowing for necessary reorganizing.

- Aquarius (approximately January 20 to February 18): Perform a ceremony to acknowledge your oneness with all of humanity. Take actions to be of service to your community. Serve food to the hungry, counsel those in need, or volunteer at a hospital. Find ways to contribute.

- Pisces (approximately February 19 to March 21): How can you cultivate spiritual practices? Which spiritual tradition are you drawn toward? Link with a tradition that comforts and inspires you. Choose a spiritual practice such as chanting, prayer, or meditation. Do this daily. Expect positive results.

Release, Renewal, and the Power of Ritual: Experiential Exercise

Every moment you have the opportunity to renew yourself, release inappropriate attachments to the past. Following these elemental guidelines, you can create rituals for your own needs.

1. Fire

Fire releases anger, limitations, and frustrations. Light a candle in a ceramic bowl, or draw a fire in your fireplace. What limitations or frustrations do you want to cast into the fire? Fire represents action. What actions do you want to be empowered to perform? Sit in front of the fire or candle, and gaze into the flames. Draw the energy of the fire into your body, strengthening your motivation to take positive actions.

2. Earth

Fill a bowl with uncooked corn or rice. Breathe deeply as you hold the bowl in front of you with gratitude to the earth. Contemplate how the earth provides you with grain for sustenance. Perhaps you can dance barefoot on the ground in the woods, at a beach, or in a park. How else do you wish to honor Mother Earth? Perhaps you can plant something. Be open to receive from the earth. Stand barefoot under a tree in order to feel the power of the earth.

3. Air

In the Native American culture, sage is known as a great purifier. Using a sage stick, or incense if you cannot find sage, purify the space around your body as well as your living and work space. As you wave the sage or incense stick around you, invoke its power to clear stagnant or dead energy. Chant a mantra, or play uplifting music. What do you wish to release? Air (wind) is the carrier of wishes, messages, and intentions. Remember the peace pipe ceremony? What wishes do you want to send into the ether? Take several deep breaths as you enjoy a long walk in nature. Consciously slow down.

4. Water

Sprinkle sea salt in a goblet or bowl filled with purified water. Gently pour this over your head, or immerse yourself in water in a bathtub, pool, or natural body of water. The spirit of water assists you in releasing sadness and disappointments. If you live near water, visit it frequently. Ask for its blessings. Listen to its messages.

Trust yourself and your imagination. Rituals can significantly aid you in renewing yourself on a regular basis…and they are fun as well!

12

Embodying the True Spirit of Giving and Receiving

Let's begin this chapter with a deep inhalation and long exhalation. Again, take a deep inhale and long exhale. Breathing is probably our most primal act of receiving moving from emptiness to fullness. While exhaling, in addition to releasing toxins, we are also emptying out, that is, clearing space, so we can receive. It goes on and on, breath by breath. Have you ever thought about that? Have you ever observed, as you listen to another person on your inhale, that you are drawing in some of his or her energy? Exhaling is an organic cleansing of any disturbing energy you have taken into your body. The breath is a very powerful vehicle for giving and receiving.

Spanda is Sanskrit for the pulsating life force energy within us. The *spanda* exists before the next breath emerges. *Spanda* is the vibration, the tingling. Whether giving or receiving, *spanda* is present. When you attain stillness in meditation, you experience *spanda*. In stillness, there is life and vibration. Now let's explore the spirit of giving.

What is the true spirit of giving?

It is your *dharma* to perform good actions. Your actions are vehicles for giving, whether they are subtle or obvious. The true spirit of giving is offering your actions to God and the universe. Before performing a good action, you can become still and silently affirm you are offering that action to God, your higher power, or the universe. Doing so, you renounce the fruit of your actions. There are no lingering expectations. As it is so eloquently stated in Yogic and Buddhist sutras, "Expectations cause suffering." When you do not receive something you are counting on, there is loss that can lead to suffering.

At times, you may want to be completely in control of your giving. You might want to refrain from giving and offering your good intentions until it feels good,

93

but, unfortunately, if you inhibit giving, it becomes your habit to hold back because your giving muscles start to atrophy. Later, while experiencing positive circumstances, you may still refrain from being generous purely out of habit.

Your intentions can be as meaningful as your actions, or even more so. When someone is not receptive to your offerings, you can still intend for this person to receive benefit by sending them wishes for love and peace. Have faith your good intentions do make a difference. I have often sent long-distance healing energy or chanted for people who were thousands of miles away. Time after time, I have received feedback that my efforts made a positive difference.

The gifts we give with high intention always bear fruit. Because of high intentions, your gifts can bring surpassing blessings to others. In the 1970s, a great swami from India gave spiritual initiation to a struggling actress in Los Angeles. As a gift, he gave her a scarf with his best intentions. Soon after, a stranger climbed in through the woman's apartment window and began raping her. She immediately began repeating the mantra the swami had given her. In the next instant, the man stopped raping her, saw the swami's scarf hanging near the bed, grabbed it, and left. The swami's *shakti* and good intentions saved her from further abuse and probably benefited her rapist as well because he now possessed a scarf brimming with the swami's *shakti*. Who knows what could happen to him?

Giving from the heart makes a positive difference whether you are composing a letter, initiating interest in someone, cooking dinner for someone, or merely saying a kind word to someone. A Manhattan man passed a homeless person daily as he left for work. One day, he decided to practice the spirit of giving with this disheveled person. With great respect, he handed the person money, praying it would greatly benefit him. The money was imbued with good intentions. The next week, he noticed the homeless man was not in his usual spot. A few days later, an immaculately dressed man in a suit enthusiastically waved to him. It was the homeless man, who approached and joyfully told him, "After you gave me the money, I felt loved. I felt like I was someone. I felt hopeful…so hopeful that I went out and found a job and a place to live!"

More about *Dharmic* Giving

Every environment you find yourself in can be sacred. With a consciousness of service, you can create more order and harmony everywhere you go, from public restrooms to litter-filled streets, hallways, parks, and forests. When you give *dharmically*, you honor the sanctity of life. You are part of the earth, and the earth is a part of you. It is everyone's *dharma* to contribute to the world, regardless of what his or her circumstances may be.

You may detest your job and spend your workday dreaming about being somewhere more pleasant instead of being right there in the moment. Many years ago, I did market research telephone surveys, coding the results with a red pencil. The coding was quite boring. As an experiment, I decided to give one hundred percent to all of my boring tasks, playing a game of total participation, as if everything really mattered to me. Pleasurable feelings instantly replaced boredom. My environment reflected my inner shift. My supervisor learned I gave Shiatsu treatments. From then on, I was allowed to give Shiatsu all day to the supervisors. At the same time, I was more in demand for Shiatsu house calls and began making a living as a healer. These amazing experiences resulted from the simple decision to be one hundred percent and fully participate in life.

How can you be present with people you can't stand?

It is frustrating to be present with people, particularly family members, who push your buttons. I have attended several family gatherings where no one even asked how I was doing or what was happening in my life. As a result, I did not attend family events for a long time. Years later, an opportunity to honor some relatives arose. Despite my resistance, I knew it was appropriate for me to attend this particular gathering. Entering the banquet hall, I gave up all my expectations. Focusing on listening to people from my heart, I saw light in everyone and resonated with everyone's higher self. No one asked me questions about my life, but I was at peace. Two years later at the next major family event, I was pleasantly surprised. These very same relatives were very loving and engaged in dialogue with me about my life. Again, I was at peace.

When you give your individual attention to others while being free of expectations, it is a vehicle for saying, "I honor the light in you." It is a very high form of giving and receiving. You can experience love and well-being with or without others' positive attention.

What about burnout from giving?

This could be a sign you are slipping into the abyss of martyrdom. This occurs when you are not *dharmic* in giving. You may sometimes give with manipulation, for example, to be liked or admired, considered indispensable, or avoid loneliness. Giving in this way leaves a bitter taste in our mouths, and it is not very pleasant to receive from someone who is manipulating either. You may have to release the expectation that someone will reward you, say he or she loves you, give you undivided attention, say he or she forgives you, or ask for your forgiveness.

It is always beneficial when you give from your heart. You can first contemplate, "Why do I feel compelled to give?" What are your expectations? At times, you perform good actions, even though you feel your heart is absent. Even so, you may feel a tingling of well-being in your body because performing a good action sometimes feels pleasurable. However, you cannot count on this.

Tell the truth about your feelings. The following are some strategies that may help if you feel burned out in giving or your heart is not present.

Strategies for Giving with Compassion

1. Pause. Breathe deeply. Feel any resentment or resistance to giving in your body. Where is it located?

2. Forgive yourself for holding on to your resentment. You are not a bad person for having these feelings.

3. Send yourself loving thoughts and affirmations. Chant, pray, or repeat your mantra.

4. If you are withholding your upset, how can you express it appropriately? Does it feel safe to tell the person directly? Is it better to write to the person or only express your feelings to him or her in your mind? What is the most appropriate action to take? Do it now.

5. Can you now give as an offering to the highest within this person, despite your differences?

6. If so, proceed, being very present.

7. If not, wait until you have either cleared or greatly diminished your upset. Then perform this action with compassion.

Blockages to Receiving

Why can't people receive the abundance of good available to them?

The bottom line is the belief, "I am not worthy." Many people receive an imprint from childhood religious training that God will not dispense his grace unless you first declare your unworthiness. The mistaken belief is that it is not spiritual to affirm your worth. If you think you are worthy of abundance, you are being arrogant and/or egotistical, that is, attitudes that invite retribution. This belief can create problems in life. For example, suppose people want to give you a birthday party, but you will not allow this acknowledgement because you believe in your unworthiness. Surely this is not right. You may be embarrassed to receive love, attention, or compliments. Perhaps attention from others is too unsettling. You might blush. Others might witness your vulnerability. You might cry or otherwise loosen your emotional armor. You may fear being perceived as soft, thus being rejected or humiliated. It may seem easier to avoid attention-getting situations than face your fears. Along with this, you may have false humility. You may present a mask to the world. "I don't need anyone. I can take care of myself." Underneath the mask, you ache to be touched, loved, and appreciated. Feelings of unworthiness can also come from guilt about past actions. When you feel guilty about something and try opening to receive grace, you sometimes only experience this guilt and do not receive spiritual blessings. Again, surely this is not right.

"Lord, I am not worthy to receive you, but only say the word and I shall be healed." To me, this means you are supposed to commune with God through your being (heart), not the ego (head). This teaching is about opening to receive grace and forgiveness, not false humility. Is it worthwhile or sensible to perpetually punish yourself for something you feel guilty about? If everything comes to you from God and the universe, then this spiritual power is alive and working through everyone and everything. You only need to look around you to receive its blessings. The smile of a stranger may encourage you to continue going when your spirits are low. A happy puppy wagging his tail reminds you that love is in the world. Flowers blooming around you in spring are a testament to perseverance during the difficult conditions of winter.

What happens if you open up and then receive criticism?

This is part of life as well. The more you are true to yourself, the more you may invite criticism from others. So what? You are at least being true to yourself. Criticism is sometimes vicious and vindictive as well as stinging and poisonous. You want to recoil in order to shake it off and cleanse yourself of this toxicity. You cannot avoid criticism in this world, but you can change your reaction to it. A saying goes, "You're damned if you do and damned if you don't." I say you should not overfocus on others' judgment of you.

How do you know if criticism is valid?

It is useful to ask yourself, "Is there a kernel of truth here?" Pretend the person is a part of you that is talking to you. Ask yourself, "What am I saying to myself?" If others say, "You are cold. You are not affectionate or interested in me," is there truth here? At the least, from that person's perspective, you seem cold and uncaring. Be willing to see his or her point of view. You do not need to agree with him or her.

Perhaps the message is to be more aware and sensitive to those around you. Sometimes, the message is to be more sensitive and caring to yourself. When criticism is abusive, cruel, or attacking, you do not have to accept it. Take a stand. Declare, "This feels abusive. I love myself and I'm not going to take it." Then leave.

How do I get rid of negative, poisonous criticism?

With the power of your intention, you can transmute the energy of negative criticism. Through chanting, prayer, and meditation with determination, the negative energy will start moving. Hatha yoga with conscious breathing as well as practicing martial arts can transmute negative energy. The MAP (Medical Assistance Program) (see the recommended reading list at the end of the book), bodywork, acupuncture, and shamanic healing can transform and release the effect of negative criticism. No one needs to be stuck with this venom.

We all have the power to be present in the now, free of negative expectations. Every moment is an opportunity to give and receive love and support.

Giving and Receiving: Experiential Exercise

1. Imagine that blue light is pouring from above your head, into your crown, and throughout your entire body.

2. Focus on being still for two minutes. Imagine you are gathering your life force energy, anchoring it in your body.

3. Imagine your right side is expanding far beyond your body. From the space of stillness, send out white light from your heart to the people in your life who you wish to love, support, and encourage. Imagine they are receiving the light from you.

4. Return to stillness for two minutes.

5. Imagine your left side is expanding way beyond your body. Imagine you are receiving all the love and support you desire from the universe in the form of a beautiful blue star. Breathe it in. Create space for it. Receive it with love and joy.

   You are now in state of balance between giving and receiving. Experience this fully.

13

Finally: How to Live Like a Monk in the World

In the summer of 1993, I met with a swami in the Siddha Yoga tradition, declaring I felt called to be a monk. Surprisingly, he responded, "Gurumayi is not accepting anymore monks. Become a monk in the world." Since that time, I have contemplated what being a monk in the world means to me. This book is the result of those contemplations.

An old paradigm from a previous era describes what is required to fully live the life of a monk. Though the paradigm is not what I have focused on in this book, I would like briefly to describe attributes of monkhood that originated thousands of years ago.

Celibacy

When you think of a traditional nun or monk, it is easy to think of celibacy. When nuns or monks are initiated into a spiritual order, they are required to be celibate. They marry God instead of another person.

Very few people can honestly claim they are completely free of sexual thoughts and desires. For the few in this category, it is natural to be celibate, focusing exclusively on service and love of God. For most of us, celibacy would be extremely unpleasant and even potentially harmful. Unless your sexual energy is transmuted into spiritual energy that revitalizes the body, many issues may emerge. Suppressed sexual desires can morph into irritability, rigidity, obsession, cruelty, and physical ailments.

If you are called to be celibate in your heart and soul, so be it. If you continue thinking about and longing for sex, then you are not yet ready to give it up. I do not believe that being celibate inherently makes you more spiritual any more than vegetarianism does. These are lifestyle choices, not necessarily enlightened ways of living.

Austerity

In convents, ashrams, and monasteries, great austerities are often practiced to accelerate spiritual purification. More moderate austerities may include a short fast or going with less sleep for a specific period. Extreme austerities may include very long fasts and regular sleep deprivation. Some orders practice self-flagellation as a form of suffering to draw one closer to God. Extreme austerities will not necessarily make you enlightened and may even be a way of avoiding the challenge that life offers every day. Every moment of your life offers the perfect option for purification in order to choose the ego or the self. Facing life and all of its drama with a conscious, loving heart, you will be more aware and alive.

Poverty

As monks and nuns leave outer society, they usually take a vow of poverty. Their new community takes care of their material needs. The belief is that total surrender to God through the spiritual order creates the experience of great abundance despite the vow of poverty. I feel we are put on this earth to be abundant beings. Poverty consciousness creates great suffering. Outside of a spiritual order, unless we are independently wealthy, we depend on our income to support us in acquiring the necessities of our lives. There is nothing wrong or unspiritual about this.

Basic Guidelines for Being a Monk in the World

1. Secure a Daily Spiritual Practice

Select a spiritual practice that resonates for you. This may include meditation, prayer, and a form of chanting. Resolve to take time every day to honor your spiritual connection. This is the greatest gift you can give yourself.

2. Keep Things in Good Order and Simplify

Make sure your home, work environment, and car are clean and in good order. We are not talking about absolute perfection here. Simply, your life will not work as well if your environments are dirty and cluttered. Regularly clear out your drawers and closets. Look for ways to simplify your life. Make sure the material things you do possess are of beauty and quality.

3.   Connect to your Environment

Wherever you are (on a crowded bus, street, a quiet garden, or huge department store), connect to your environment. Look for beauty around you in people, nature, and objects. Take time to take it all in.

4.   Be More Present, Kind, and Loving

As you connect to your environment, do not dwell on your thoughts and worries. Slow down your thinking. Be more present with those around you. Express kindness wherever you go. Silently bless everyone and everything around you, including animals, trees, and flowers. Especially bless people who make you uncomfortable.

5.   Respect Yourself

Do not speak ill of yourself. Never put yourself down. As you choose your foods, beverages, and exercise regime, step back and look at yourself as you would someone you love very much. Make sure this person is taking great care of himself or herself.

6.   Respect Others and All of Nature

Do not invest your energy in bad-mouthing and putting down others. You do not need to like everyone, but why put out a critical, judgmental energy toward others? Is that what you want to attract? Extend yourself to pick up litter and create greater beauty in your neighborhood. Be mindful of people around you. Do not pollute your environment with cigarette or cigar smoke, loud music, or very loud conversations. Your actions affect everyone and everything around you.

7.   Outflow Continuously and Be More Abundant

Share positive energy everywhere you go. Smile at strangers. Bless them silently. Acknowledge beauty, generosity, and good deeds. When you receive good service, be extra generous with your gratuity. Spend each day in the spirit of *seva*, selfless service. As long as they are receptive, outflow lessons you have learned, realizations, experiences, and pleasures with others.

8. Spend Quality Time Alone

Claim quiet time alone daily. Retreat, renew, and contemplate your life. Release upsets from the past, and renew yourself with enthusiasm for the future.

9. Surround Yourself with Inspiration

Keep beautiful objects and photos that inspire you around your home and work space. Listen daily to music that lifts your spirits. Read uplifting books. Choose inspiring plays and films. Refrain from contact with the negative, violent, and sensational. Focus on people who are vibrating on high energy in their lives. You can do it, too! You can contribute this to the world.

In Closing

Dear Friends,

Thank you for allowing me to share my experiences and knowledge with you. May you receive great benefit from the spiritual strategies and be inspired to perform good actions and share your creativity with the world. We are all spiritual beings. Let us respect our differences and discover our similarities.

In this moment, you can make great spiritual progress in exactly the life circumstances you find yourself. May everyone attain enlightenment and joy.

Love and Shanti,
Richard Damien

Recommended Reading

Chia, Mantak and Douglas Abrams. *The Multi Orgasmic Male.* Harper Press, SF.
Hochswender, Woody, Greg Martin, and Ted Marino. *The Buddha in Your Mirror.* Middleway Press.
Rosenberg, Marshall. *Non-Violent Communication.* Puddle Dancer Press.
Small, Machelle. *M.A.P. (Medical Assistance Program).* Wright Perelandra Press.
Swami Chidvilasanada. *The Yoga of Discipline.* Syda Foundation.
Tolle, Eckhart. *The Power of Now.* New World Library.
Wolcott, William and Trish Fahey. *The Metabolic Type Diet.* Broadway Books.

For information about Richard Damien's workshops, lectures, events, and CDs, contact:

www.richarddamien.com

978-0-595-37608-7
0-595-37608-8

63505252R00077

Made in the USA
Lexington, KY
09 May 2017